The Service User as a Partner in Social Work
Projects and Education

Emanuela Chiapparini (ed.)

The Service User as a Partner in Social Work Projects and Education

Concepts and Evaluations of Courses with a Gap-Mending Approach in Europe

Barbara Budrich Publishers
Opladen • Berlin • Toronto 2016

All rights reserved. No part of this publication may be reproduced, stored in or introduced into a retrieval system, or transmitted, in any form, or by any means (electronic, mechanical, photocopying, recording or otherwise) without the prior written permission of Barbara Budrich Publishers. Any person who does any unauthorized act in relation to this publication may be liable to criminal prosecution and civil claims for damages.

You must not circulate this book in any other binding or cover and you must impose this same condition on any acquirer.

A CIP catalogue record for this book is available from
Die Deutsche Bibliothek (The German Library)

© 2016 by Barbara Budrich Publishers, Opladen, Berlin & Toronto
www.barbara-budrich.net

ISBN 978-3-8474-0507-8
eISBN 978-3-8474-0929-8

Das Werk einschließlich aller seiner Teile ist urheberrechtlich geschützt. Jede Verwertung außerhalb der engen Grenzen des Urheberrechtsgesetzes ist ohne Zustimmung des Verlages unzulässig und strafbar. Das gilt insbesondere für Vervielfältigungen, Übersetzungen, Mikroverfilmungen und die Einspeicherung und Verarbeitung in elektronischen Systemen.

Die Deutsche Bibliothek – CIP-Einheitsaufnahme
Ein Titeldatensatz für die Publikation ist bei der Deutschen Bibliothek erhältlich.

Verlag Barbara Budrich ⓑ Barbara Budrich Publishers
Stauffenbergstr. 7. D-51379 Leverkusen Opladen, Germany

86 Delma Drive. Toronto, ON M8W 4P6 Canada
www.barbara-budrich.net

Jacket illustration by Bettina Lehfeldt, Kleinmachnow, Germany –
www.lehfeldtgraphic.de
Copy Edit: Máiréad Collins, Belfast, UK
Typesetting: R + S, Redaktion + Satz Beate Glaubitz, Leverkusen
Printed in Europe on acid-free paper by paper&tinta, Warsaw

This book project could be implemented thanks to the support of the Institute of Child, Youth and Family (School of Social Work) at the Zurich University of Applied Sciences.

Contents

Index for tables and figures 7

Foreword 9

1. **Introduction: Service User Involvement – Social Work Projects and Education with a Gap-Mending Approach in Europe** 13
   Emanuela Chiapparini

2. **Service User Involvement – Social Work Projects and Education with Gap-Mending Approach in Europe** 25
   Overview of the Theoretical Background and of the Evaluation
   Emanuela Chiapparini

3. **Examples of courses in Europe** 37

   3.1 Sweden: Power, Experiences and Mutual Development. Using The Concept of Gap-Mending in Social Work Education 37
   Arne Kristiansen and Cecilia Heule

   3.2 Norway: Do Gap-Mending Methods Have any Long-Term Effects? Experiences from the Norwegian Course 'Meeting Face to Face Creates Insights' 54
   Liv Altmann, Tove Hasvold and Ole Petter Askheim

3.3 England: Gap-Mending: Developing a New Approach to User and Carer Involvement in Social Work Education 69
Peter Beresford, Helen Casey and John MacDonough

3.4 Denmark: Interdisciplinary Gap-Mending Courses as Part of R&D Projects at the Metropolitan University College 88
Ann Rasmussen and Camusa Hatt

3.5 Germany: Service User Involvement at Esslingen University of Applied Sciences: Background, Concept and Experiences 106
Thomas Heidenreich and Marion Laging

3.6 Switzerland: First Approaches on an Implementation of Courses with a Gap-Mending Approach 124
Véronique Eicher and Emanuela Chiapparini

4. **Conclusion: Empowering Service Users and Innovative Learning Settings with Long-Term Effects** 133
Emanuela Chiapparini

The contributors 141

Index for tables and figures

3.1
Figure 1. Three ways to attend the Mobilisation Course at the School of Social Work at Lund University in Sweden 44

Figure 2. Course outline of the Mobilisation Course at the School of Social Work at Lund University in Sweden 46

Table 1. Number of students on the Mobilisation Course at the School of Social Work at Lund University in Sweden 50

3.5
Table 1. Areas of qualification according to the Qualification Framework for Social Work 107

Table 2. Overview of project seminars and SUI seminars conducted at Esslingen University of Applied Sciences 114

Table 3. Contents and methods of SUI seminar I 116

Foreword

My family and I have been service users for almost 40 years. I am 45 years old and a mother of four boys between the ages of 3 and 28 years. I am a client, patient, service user and a carer. I have been active in different service user organisations for 30 years, and have listened to the life stories of other service users. There have been stories about sickness, poverty, substance abuse, mental health problems, vulnerable parents due to disabilities and a variety of social or psychological problems. I do not have any vocational training or higher education.

When I first got in contact with lecturers working at the School of Social Work at the University of Lund, I dare say that I had a service user perspective. However, only when I became a student, and later a tutor at the Mobilisation course (cf. Chapter 3.1), did I fully understand the meaning of a service user perspective and the consequences of inequality regarding power distribution in social work practice.

The subjects dealt with in the courses were related to everyone's own life experiences. It was important to grasp the difference between "experience" and "knowledge". Both can be valuable for others. Everything I have experienced, for example as a former foster care child, as a drug addict or as a parent of children with disabilities is not an abstract knowledge without practical references. On the other hand, neither is it about exposing yourself without any limits. The point is to find significant examples taken from your personal experience so that others can learn something important from those.

I am convinced that social workers need to understand the perspectives of service users, or clients, in order to understand how paralysing oppressive practises can be for them. Only when social workers and service users can meet on a more equal ground, can social work become more sustainable and meaningful. Perhaps we can learn the importance of our own and other experiences – in a gap-mending way – across boundaries and through linking with work that is taking place in other countries and in different societies.

The Mobilisation course in Lund is unique. It has led to a number of valuable networks and collaborations. In my case, it helped me start a national service user organisation working for parents who had their children placed in foster care. The name of the organisation is Maskrosföräldrar[1]. Maskros is the Swedish word for dandelion. In Sweden the dandelion is known for its strength and resilience, a plant that can bloom even in the middle of an asphalt road. The expression 'dandelion child' is already commonly used to refer to young people growing up under hard circumstances. And we hope that our children will grow up to a better life than the one of their parents.

I started this association in 2013 and it has now grown to about 160 members, in addition to a large number of non-member parents that we are in contact. Our purpose is, besides offering support to individuals, to influence political decisions and to disseminate knowledge about the needs of our members. Our focal argument is that (...) no parent has a right to their child(ren), but all children have a right to a parent. In recent years, we have been running projects in collaboration with different NGOs (e.g. "Swedish Association of Local Authorities and Regions"), the School of Social Work in Lund, with national authorities and Swedish municipalities. In one of these projects, we visited members of the network PowerUs (cf. Chapter 1) in Durham in the North of England, where parents like ourselves were taking part in a course led by Helen Casey. I also participated in the European Association of School of Social Work (EASSW) conference in Milan last summer. My presentation "How to Empower a Collapsed Parenthood" received a great deal of positive feedback and my network of interested lecturers and researchers has since then increased further.

When people, who have been earlier separated by different gaps in society, start to share their perspectives with each other, is more fruitful. My organisation is proof of this and this book is as well. I hope that service users and social work students and lecturers can make this necessary paradigm shift in social work practice quickly with the objective of creating a more valuable society for everybody. This includes people with greater difficulties and obstacles than most of the others who are more privileged. Europe is fac-

---

1   Further information about the user organisation "Maskrosföräldrar" can be found on: www.maskrosforaldrar.se. Cited: 2016-01-11.

ing great difficulties and I believe there is no better way than to contribute our share in building partnerships with each other.

Borås (Sweden), 28.1.2016
Malin Widerlöv
Founder and chairwoman
of the service user organisation Maskrosföräldrar

1. Introduction: Service User Involvement – Social Work Projects and Education with a Gap-Mending Approach in Europe

Emanuela Chiapparini

In order to become a competent social worker, it is essential to know the perspective of the service users[1]. Therefore, the International Federation of Social Workers (IFSW) developed a European framework for quality assurance of the social profession (Anghel/Ramon 2009), where the involvement of service users became a key element in social work practice and education (Jones/Radulescu 2006). The role of social workers was adapted to the needs of service users. In other countries, such as Brazil, Canada, Israel and the USA, it is common to involve service users in social work education (Shor/Sykes 2002). In the United Kingdom, the involvement of service users as consultants in social work education (in teaching, selection, admission, assessment of students) has been a mandatory requirement since 2003 (Anghel/Ramon 2009: 186). Generally, service users are more and more included in practice, research and education of social work in different European countries (Schön 2015, 2016). However, in social work practice, research and education, they are usually reduced to the role of information providers and do not actively take part as co-partners or co-researchers (e.g. Beresford/Carr 2012). Furthermore, debates about the involvement of service users are more common in Northern European countries than in German-speaking countries. Nevertheless, there are hardly any publications that explore and reflect the involvement of service users in courses of social work education. For the first

---

1 People using social services are called "service users", "clients", "customers" or "experts of experience" in the literature based on different arguments that will be discussed in Chapter 2. It will also be explained why the term "service user" is used in this book and how it is defined.

time, this anthology gives an overview of different courses in social work education in European countries, in which service users are included as partners. The main characteristic of these courses is that service users and students of social work share their experiences, they study and work together. They do this, as far as possible, on an equal level by using the gap-mending approach.

Gap-Mending Approach

Mending the gap is a valuable new approach to professional learning and academic teaching (c.f. Chapter 3.1).

The approach was launched in 2012 as the network PowerUs[2] developed a joint vision to mend gaps between social workers and service users in social work education. PowerUs worked at that time with two strategies (Heule/Kristiansen 2013: 15): First with a gap-mending approach to courses and second with gap-mending as a UK strategy of mainstreaming service user participation.

The courses with a gap-mending approach in social work education (Heule/Kristiansen 2013: 4) aim in the first place to empower socially excluded groups. The first strategy consists of joint courses, where social work students study together with students from service user organisations (Heule/Kristiansen 2013: 4). The second strategy was developed in the UK, where service user participation was mainstreamed and requested in all levels of decision making in social work education. The joint courses aims to empower both the social work students and the students from service user organisations that often have been socially excluded in society.

Secondly, the aim of the courses is that the students meet the service users in a situation out of their "role as a social worker" on common ground. This enables a learning process that is based on exploring their needs and views.

Thirdly, during the course, both service users and social workers develop innovative projects together in the field of social work.

---

2 Further information about the international network PowerUs can be found on: http://powerus.se/ or in the film"Mend the gap – A challenge for social work education" (2015): https://www.youtube.com/watch?v=QExM_aA2Mus&feature=youtu.be. Cited: 2016-01-11.

Social workers learn from service users and vice versa, which requires that service users recognise their knowledge, but also their limitations and that they value their experience and knowledge (Beresford 2000: 500-501). These are the central elements, which guarantee that service users do not only have the role of information providers but are really co-partners in courses of social work education.

Up to now, courses with a gap-mending approach have been conducted in and adapted to several European countries, e.g. Sweden, England, Norway, Denmark, Germany and Switzerland.

Lecturers, tutors, representatives of service user organisations and researchers from these countries are connected through the international network "PowerUs". PowerUs organises exchange meetings to develop the mainstreaming of service user participation. Further, they enhance visits to discuss the latest findings and to promote courses with a gap-mending approach. They also take part in national and international social work conferences to actively promote both courses with a gap-mending approach and the mainstreaming of service user participation.

The Structure of the Book

The aim of this book is to describe several courses with a gap-mending approach in social work education in Europe. Therefore, the main part of this book comprises the presentation, evaluation and discussion of examples of six countries, which are structured into six contributions. The book starts with an introductory chapter for clarifying the range of theoretical approaches of gap-mending methods. It discusses three key terms: user involvement, service user/service user organisations and empowerment. This does not resolve the theoretical challenges with a gap-mending approach, but it stresses the strengths and limitations of these challenges. At the same time, it becomes clear that social workers have to collaborate with service users and understand their personal background. This is easier said than done. One solution would be that they attend courses with a gap-mending approach, where service users and social workers learn and work together on an equal level as far as possible.

The book links experience with user involvement and gap-mending in English-speaking and German-speaking countries. It invites the reader to become familiar with different implementations of courses using a gap-mending approach in various European countries. The courses were developed and adapted to each country's educational system for social workers, their society's needs and circumstances. There is for instance one course that has already taken place 18 times and is based on a long-standing experience. Other courses have only just gained their first experiences. By presenting such a variety of courses, this book offers an insight into different states and conditions of courses with a gap-mending approach. In addition, each contribution reflects and evaluates the implementations of the gap-mending approach and reveals new perspectives for future development.

In order to provide a better orientation for the reader, all the presented examples of courses with a gap-mending approach underlie the same structure:

context of the course
concept of the course
realisation and implementation of the course
evaluation and critical reflections.

The authors of this anthology have developed and have taught courses in social work education with a gap-mending approach. Additionally, most of them work in user-involved research and practice. Furthermore, they are all part of the international network PowerUs.

Sweden: Power, Experiences and Mutual Development. Using The Concept of Gap-Mending in Social Work Education:
Arne Kristiansen and Cecilia Heule

The authors of this first chapter, Kristiansen and Heule, focus on the initial concept of courses with a gap-mending approach in the school of social work at the Lund University in Sweden. The first six-week course called "Mobilization Course" started in 2005. In this course, students of social work and students from service user organizations studied and developed a project together on an equal level as much as possible. Up until today, it has been carried out 18 times and 626 students (205 students from service user organizations, 398 bachelor students and 23 master students of social work) have completed this course.

The authors firstly explain the term "gap-mending" by pointing out the theoretical discussion about both the power of social workers in front of service users and their discriminations of the structure of social services. In this setup, the social worker is the expert and the service users are often seen as the problem. With Hasenfeld (1992), the authors argue for a "redistribution of power" in social work practice, where service users obtain more power over their lives. Further, the authors highlight the concept of gap-mending, which is more an analytical approach and less a model or a method. The aim of this approach consists in enabling a mutual learning between service users and students of social work for resolving social problems. The chapter offers the pedagogic reflections and the experiences made with the mobilising course, which shows an important and an effective opportunity to start a process of building a relationship between service users and social workers.

The users' perspective is addressed in the Swedish social work education at university level in at least one course. However, Kristiansen and Heule pointed out some elements of development for these courses to guarantee an increase of continuing partnership and a learning process between lecturer, students and people who represent different service users' interests.

The authors discuss some challenges of the course and underline the positive evaluation of students' discussions during the course. The students' feedback (including social work students and service user students) was gathered by means of a questionnaire and written reflections at the end of each course. The success of the course is confirmed due to the fact some of the service user students were subsequently invited to attend other courses to share their experiences. Other service user students have even started new user organisations. Several concepts of their projects received funds to implement them in social work practice. Finally, the authors have been invited to national and international meetings and congresses to speak about their work. They are a vital partner in the development of the international network PowerUs.

Norway: Do Gap-Mending Methods Have any Long-Term Effects? Experiences from the Norwegian Course 'Meeting Face to Face Creates Insights':
Liv Altmann, Tove Hasvold and Ole Petter Askheim

The authors, Liv Altmann, Tove Hasvold and Ole Petter Askheim, present an evaluation of a three-week course called "Meeting Face to Face Creates Insights". The course took place for the first time in 2009 at the Lillehammer University College (LUC) and the course was subsequently repeated six times with a total of 189 students: 68 service users (external students) and 121 internal bachelor students. In Norway and other countries, these courses are new. Usually, the students either meet service users during their internship or service users are invited to the university as guest speakers. Owing to this setup, the courses with gap-mending methods in Norway have a good basis for being evaluated in the long term. The authors carried out such an evaluation with former external and internal students. The results of this evaluation show long-term outcomes, which the authors discuss under five headlines.

Regarding the positive long-term outcomes, the authors propose that such courses should be organized for all students. Further, the service users (external students) and the social work students (internal students) are regarded as valuable contributors to a change in social work practice, which entails more than just expressing respect and tolerance towards each other. Finally, the authors give important advice on organizing and implementing successful courses.

England: Gap-Mending: Developing a New Approach to User and Carer Involvement in Social Work Education:
Peter Beresford, Helen Casey and John MacDonough

This chapter takes account of the history of social work in the UK. In the British history of social work, both the regulation of charity and commitment to social citizenship as well as the equalization of opportunity have always been emphasized. The authors, Beresford, Casey and MacDonough, explain with a historical overview, the vanguard development of social work and why user involvement in policy and practice was established already in the 1990s. Since 2003, user involvement in social work education has been compulsory. However, the first courses with gap-mending methods were introduced at the London South Bank University (LSBU) in 2012 and at New College Durham (NCD) in 2014. The authors explain the different developments of both courses, which show the importance of considering the needs of the single university context. At LSBU, the delivery of the 12-week module with sessions once a week called "Advocacy, Partnership and Participation" was supported by professional regulatory bodies. This chapter shows the importance of the refinement of the concept of the module, revealed by an initial research study, which was conducted with a focus group of service users and bachelor students of social work. The authors report the results of the study. In a very different way, the first gap-mending course at NCD was initiated by a practice organisation and by service users in order to close the gap between social workers and service users. The authors explain how they developed the programme of the course in nine meetings. Further, the chapter explores the successful implementation of this gap-mending methodology pilot project. Nine parents (seven mothers and two fathers) ran the course and eight students of social work and one of community health participated in it. The authors highlight the mainly positive aspects and mention only one that is negative, which was the inadequate service of provision and support. The authors stressed that both programmes had a positive influence on other programmes and co-operations in social work education. Finally, the chapter makes an important contribution to the ongoing political, ideological and academic discussions in the UK. The authors consider the gap-mending approach as an evidence-based alternative to the ongoing regressive direction of understanding social work. They argue that the gap-mending approach is of international interest and it has to be linked to the roots of social work in the UK.

Denmark: Interdisciplinary Gap-Mending Courses as Part of R&D Projects at the Metropolitan University College:
Ann Rasmussen and Camusa Hatt

The focus of the chapter of Ann Rasmussen and Camusa Hatt is on the important role that gap-mending methods play in local innovation projects formed as interdisciplinary courses in the bachelor curriculum of social work, nursing, occupational therapy and other welfare studies at the Metropolitan University College in Denmark. This university college has offered several courses with service user involvement. However, the presented courses have in common that they are innovation projects focussing on one specific practice challenge with one user group previously identified by Metropolitan and confirmed by service providers. Further, users, students and volunteers work as co-creators of new ideas and solutions, whereas service providers participate as guests or clients.

Different from the previous chapters, the authors of this chapter apply the abbreviated term "user" and not the term service user in order to emphasize the wider user context. They discuss two six-week courses, which provide new solutions to two specific and current welfare challenges. The first course aimed at offering new services or at the improvement of existing services for the increasing number of Danish veterans with serious psychological injuries. The second course focused on new or improved health initiatives for refugees and immigrants from non-western countries living in social housing estates. The chapter highlights the different steps of the development of each course and how difficulties, as for example recruiting service users, were resolved. The authors explain how the structure of each course was adapted to the practice issue. The first course was conducted with eight service users and 12 students from six different welfare study programmes (including social work, nursing and occupational therapy). They started by spending two days together in a rural setting in order to get acquainted. Afterwards, they worked in smaller groups. 40 users participated in the second project, which consisted of four workshops, some of which took place in the social housing estates on Fridays after the mosque prayers. The authors discuss the challenges that the interdisciplinary team of students and teachers had to face. They also underline how the second course was based on the experience of the first one. Both projects had a great positive effect and impact on the users, students and providers.

Germany: Service User Involvement at Esslingen University of Applied Sciences: Background, Concept and Experiences: Thomas Heidenreich and Marion Laging

In their chapter, Thomas Heidenreich and Marion Laging present their experiences with service user involvement seminars at Esslingen University of Applied Sciences. The description of the approach developed in Esslingen is embedded in a presentation of social work education in Germany including a brief historical sketch. Only in recent decades, social work has been regarded as an academic discipline, although with few systematic contact approaches with service users or the popular self-help groups. Against this background, the authors reveal the successful implementation of the approach of user involvement in the existing bachelor module called "student project". Within this module, they developed a two-semester course inspired by the early work of the PowerUs network. There, lecturers design a project with the students, in which service users are included. A special feature of the Esslingen approach is that students collaborate actively and in a participatory way in shaping the formats, choosing possible participants and themes for the service user seminars. The first group of eight students started after this preparatory work in 2014 with the aim to answer the crucial question "What is good social work?"'. A two-day seminar was held with service users from the field of mental illness and addiction. The output was a DVD containing the service users' answers to the question above. Based on this first experience, the second project started in 2015 using the same participatory inclusion of students. It concentrated on people with mental health service experiences including participants from EX-IN training (Experienced Involvement) which shows a large overlap in aims and approaches to user involvement. Both students and lecturers organized a meeting for service users who had taken part in previous courses as well as for lecturers who teach mental health. Two further projects were run during the same time. The first two projects mentioned above involved 26 students and 30 service users. The detailed report and evaluation of both show positive effects. On the one hand, they enabled students to experience in-depth discussions with service users on an eye-to-eye level and on the other hand, EX-IN graduates were introduced to the university setting. The authors conclude their chapter by outlining further possibilities for developing this concept in their department as well as for user involvement approaches in general. They mention the important challenges that have to be faced in the future.

Switzerland: First Approaches on an Implementation of Courses with a Gap-Mending Approach:
Véronique Eicher and Emanuela Chiapparini

The chapter of Eicher and Chiapparini first explores the situation of service user organizations and user involvement in Switzerland. The authors note that there are not many examples of user involvement in the field of social work, even though self-help groups are quite prevalent in Switzerland. They present some exceptional projects of user involvement in the domain of mental health, in the prevention of substance abuse and in the field of poverty. In social work education, internships, visits to social services and the involvement of service users for individual talks or presentations are well established. However, service users are not really involved in the development of courses and do not normally participate for the duration of an entire course. Against this background, the focus of this chapter is to present the first steps of implementing a course with the gap-mending approach in social work education at the Zurich University of Applied Sciences. The authors present the concept of a three-day course at the bachelor degree level with the title "Empowerment in Social

Work: Encounters of Students and Service Users without the Official and Contractual Relationship". It is inspired by the courses of the Lund University. The authors have also evaluated a first introduction to the topic of service user involvement in an ongoing master degree module. This chapter is helpful for readers who are interested in implementing a course with the gap-mending approach in social work education, where such an approach is less known.

In the third chapter, the conclusions highlight common issues and main elements along with differences between all examples. It draws back to the theoretical background and gives some perspectives.

This book presents the implementation of different courses of user involvement with a gap-mending approach and shows why those courses are such an important element of social work education. It also reveals the challenges that can be met and how they may be tackled. Additionally, this book would like to invite the reader to apply this approach by offering a broad overview of implementations of courses in European countries. It takes different political, educational and economical frameworks into consideration. The contributions present helpful suggestions and stimulate further implementations. Finally, the book aims to intensify the discussions about service user involvement in the education of social work in English and German-speaking countries.

References

Anghel, Roxana; Ramon, Shula (2009): Service users and carers' involvement in social work education: lessons from an English case study. In: *European Journal of Social Work* 12 (2), pp. 185-199.
Beresford, P. (2000): Service users' knowledges and social work theory: conflict or collaboration? In: *British Journal of Social Work* 30 (4), pp. 489-503.
Beresford, Peter (2012): The Theory and Philosophy Behind User Involvement. In: Beresford, Peter; Carr, Sarah (Hg.) (2012): *Social care, service users and user involvement*. London: Jessica Kingsley Publishers, pp. 19-36.
Beresford, Peter; Carr, Sarah (Hg.) (2012): *Social care, service users and user involvement*. London: Jessica Kingsley Publishers.
Hasenfeld, Yeshekel (1992): Power in Social Work Practice. In: Hasenfeld, Yeheskel (red.) *Human services as complex organizations*. London: Sage.
Heule, Cecilia; Kristiansen, Arne (2013): *Mend the gap – a teaching method for a mobilising social work*. Lund University. Lund. Retrieved on 29.12.2015 from:

http://powerus.se/wp-content/uploads/10092-Broschyr-Gapmending-engelsk-version.pdf.

Jones, D.N. and Radulescu, A., 2006. Regional perspectives from Europe. In: *International Social Work*, 49 (3), pp. 412-418.

PowerUs (2016): PowerUs. The Social Work Learning Partnership. Retrieved 27.1.2016 from: http://www.powerus.se/.

Schön, Ulla-Karin (2015): User Involvement in Social Work and Education-A Matter of Participation? In: *Journal of evidence-informed social work*, pp. 1-13.

Schön, Ulla-Karin (2016): User Involvement in Social Work and Education-A Matter of Participation? In: *Journal of evidence-informed social work* 13 (1), pp. 21-33.

Shor, R. and Sykes, I., 2002. Introducing structured dialogue with people with mental illness into the training of social work students. In: *Journal of Psychiatric Rehabilitation*, 26 (1), pp. 63-69.

2. Service User Involvement – Social Work Projects and Education with a Gap-Mending Approach in Europe

Emanuela Chiapparini

Overview of Theoretical Background and Evaluation

Theoretical Background

The gap-mending approach is based on the user involvement approach. There is general consensus that the theoretical background has not been concisely and systematically compiled until now (e.g. Askheim 2003). It can be observed that authors writing about user involvement refer implicitly or explicitly in quite different ways to empowerment, inclusion, participation, democracy, social movements, intersectionality and capability (as e.g. Schön 2015; Beresford/Carr 2012; Beresford 2013; McLaughlin 2009). However, these authors point out that the theoretical references have many common points and are difficult to define precisely in contrast to each other. Therefore, it is difficult to clearly delineate the theoretical frame of the gap-mending approach. These authors conclude that it would be advisable to differentiate between different backgrounds and individuals.

However, the user involvement approach and gap-mending approach are situated in the same theoretical paradigm of social work, which is known as critical or reflective social work. This theoretical understanding of social work is present in both English (Fook 2012; Fook 2002) and German-speaking countries (Dewe/Otto 2012; Dewe 2009; Dewe/Otto 1996) and includes a paradigm shift of social work, where the role and perspective of service users gain crucial importance (cf. next section). Social work in practice, education and research is seen as a reconstructive reality and therefore it cannot be understood well enough with a more objective or standardized approach. Thus, an active participation of service users in practice, research and education of social work and an ensuing look at their perspective will increase the understanding of their situations.

Researchers highlight the following characteristics of the user involvement approach (c.f. as e.g. Beresford/Carr 2012; Schön 2015; McLaughlin 2009):

- the understanding of single life situations
- the success of co-operation between service users and social workers
- the decrease of the power hierarchy
- the development of innovative and sustainable programs.

There are points of similarity in theoretical approaches in both English and German-speaking publications.

In the following sub-chapter, the strengths and limitations of three relevant terms of user involvement, service users and empowerment are presented.

User Involvement

The term "user involvement" is often used without definition. Schön (2016) confirms this in her systematic analysis of 699 scientific articles about user involvement (in practice and in education of social work) published between 2007 and 2013. She found that user involvement was implicitly linked to a power dimension and the hierarchy of control in McLaughlin's work (McLaughlin 2009). However, the common term user involvement was not defined in detail (Schön 2016: 27). In general, it seems to be self-evident that the term is comprehensible, clear and correct, when this is far from true (Beresford/Carr 2012; Schön 2016: 27). The definition of user involvement has "to be considered more carefully" (Beresford/Carr 2012: 27). Before trying to define it, both authors emphasise the importance of linking the user involvement approach to an ideological, political and cultural context. This way, the concept cannot be used in every situation. This "technical" application of user involvement can be avoided by outlining the implicit context of "politics and political philosophy; democracy and power; of citizenship rights and responsibilities" (Beresford/Carr 2012: 21). However, the term is often separated from these contexts and "treated in isolation as a technical rather than ideological matter" (ebd.).

Schön (2016) argues in a similar way: The complexity of defining the concept of user involvement is due to the fact that it is underpinned by issues of power, culture and politicisation. In this sense, Schön explains that "the concept of user involvement and arguments around it can be related to three areas, namely, democracy (Dahlberg/Vedung 2001), power and empowerment, and service development (McLaughlin 2011)" (Schön 2016: 22). Beresford and Carr also stress the key terms of participation and power. They see the access and support of participation and power as two important components to achieve successful involvement (Beresford/Carr 2012: 29). The challenge is to involve more service users in practice, education and research of social work. This is usually an external initiative coming from the social workers' side. However, they can only create favourable framework conditions for self-empowerment, but ultimately, the motivation needs to come from the service users themselves. Beresford and Carr call this challenge the "ambiguity of user involvement" and they explain it as follows: "keeping power from people – to hold on to power or to share it." (Beresford/Carr 2012: 31).

Already in 1997, Forbes and Sashidharan mentioned the complexities and contradictions of user involvement (Forbes/Sashidharan 1997). They observe a substitution of the concept of empowerment with the concept of user involvement and a danger of covering up the challenges and critical points of both concepts. The asymmetrical relationship between service providers and service users, for example, could be ignored (ibid.: 484). Further, the danger of user involvement linked to community care could concern the staff more than the users (ibid.). The awareness of these misunderstandings concerning the concept of user involvement provides a better understanding of the next two sections.

Despite this criticism, the concept of user involvement is widely used in the field of social work. However, there are different levels of intensity of the practice of user involvement. Usually, the role of service user is that of a consultant, for example during the research process and for the interpretation of the findings (Cossar/Neil 2015). There is hardly ever complete involvement in research work, although the service user should actually take control of the research (Beresford 2013). Furthermore, Beresford and Boxall (2012) demand a "collective involvement of service users" in education and research of social work (ibid.: 164-165). They argue that service users and service user organisations together have a stronger influence on promoting the understanding of user involvement. They can offer more direct information about studies made by service users themselves and about their own understanding. The manner of involvement depends on the understanding of the role of service users, which will be revealed in the next sub-chapter.

"Service User" and Service User Organisations

In the previous sub-chapter, it was seen that the theoretical paradigm shift of social work, known as critical or reflective social work, has had an influence on the practice of social work and the active role of the "service user". Service users are defined as givers, not only as takers and as active participants, rather than passive recipients (Anghel/Ramon 2009: 187).

The term service user has had a tradition of 40 years in the service system in Britain (Beresford 2005). The term goes back to groups who use the term "to secure their rights and needs in relation to their use of health, social care and welfare policies and services" (ibid.: 469).

Further, the Directorate General for Employment, Social Affairs and Equal Opportunities of the European Commission (2010) assigns service users an important active role, in contrast to viewing them as an "object" that needs treatment and social protection:

> "A 'paradigm shift' in attitude and approach towards the role and position of service users in SSGI [Social Services of General Interest] can be identified. In this new attitude and approach, service users of SSGI have not been viewed as 'objects' of charity, medical treatment, caretaking and social protection. Rather they are considered and viewed as persons with rights who are able to (or should be supported to) claim those rights and make decisions in their lives based on free and informed consent as well as being active members of society. The new attitude and approach to service users is expressed in human rights conventions and declarations and has substantial consequences for quality concepts used in the provision of social services: the recognition of persons served in making choices and having control over their own life." (Directorate General for Employment, Social Affairs and Equal Opportunities of the European Commission 2010: 5-6)

In the course of the re-evaluation of the active role of service users, other terms are used, such as patient, client and customer. They are seen as inappropriate since they have a more oppressive character in contrast to the term service user (Beresford/Carr 2012: 27). Admittedly, the term service user itself has implications and weaknesses (Beresford 2005: 471; McLaughlin 2009; Beresford/Carr 2012: 12-13; Beresford 2012: 27-29):

- It implies a passive attitude.
- It implies an economic understanding of social work.

- It focuses on an unspecified person and not on a relationship between a social worker and person in a specific social situation.
- It labels people and reduces their identity to the consumption of the public services.
- It reduces the complex identities that people may have and implies that all those people have something in common.
- It ignores that many service users are involuntary service users and compelled to use services.
- It has negative connotations of manipulating or "using" people.
- It includes people who do not want access to services.

Furthermore, some service users reject the term "service user" and instead prefer the term "consultant" (Anghel/Ramon 2009).

McLaughlin (2009) has also criticised other similar terms. He mentions that the alternative term "expert of experience" is not adequate. The reason is that the people cannot "differentiate between the nature and types of experience" within their own experiences (ibid.: 1113-1114).

It seems that there is no adequate term. Nevertheless, the term service user will be used in this book – with the awareness of its limitations and weaknesses – due to the fact that it is frequently used in national and international debates of social policies, social services and social work research. Furthermore, it has been used both by social systems and by service users together within their organisations. Perhaps, as suggested by Beresford (2005), the term service user "serves as a route to transforming or even ending the status of 'service user'" (Beresford 2005: 475).

However, both McLaughlin (2009) and Beresford (2005) appeal to social workers to reflect on the appropriateness of the term. Language is not neutral. It conveys hidden meanings and concepts, which have an influence on social interactions in social work.

Similar discussions about language and the term service user are going on in the German-speaking context with the German term "Adressaten" ("addressees") of social work (cf. Thiersch 2013). Pointing to the theoretical background, Thiersch presents a historical review starting with Rousseau's concept that children are basically good, and continuing to the movement of democracy, justice and emancipation. Thiersch refers to human rights and explains that service users have the right to a life with dignity (Thiersch 2013: 20). He postulates that every citizen has to be empowered for participation in society and emphasises the following conditions (ibid.: 29):

Social workers have to be aware of the fact that they are influenced by the institutional framework. They have to clarify their point of view.

Both their work objectives and the institutional framework have to be determined precisely in team meetings and supervisions. In the course of these meetings, it is important to work out the biographical influence of every individual social worker.

It is important to trust and provide space for service users, so that they can express their concerns without any fear of consequences.

An institutional acknowledgement of the important role of service users is crucial. This implies that neither the form of participation of service users, nor their right to contact an ombudsman should have any negative consequences.

These conditions have to be guaranteed and promoted by social workers. In addition, it is important to be aware of the complexity and variety of the service users' involvement in social work.

In this context, service user organisations play a very important role, too. To our knowledge, there are hardly any service user organisations active in the field of social work in contrast to the field of psychology or psychiatry in Germany and Switzerland (cf. Chapter 3.6). The situation is quite different in English-speaking countries. In Britain, for instance, there is the very active and well-known service user organisation "Shaping Our Lives" (2015). It is an independent, national user-controlled organisation in the field of health and social care. They encourage and develop effective user involvement on a local and international level. They also provide a clear and comprehensive definition of the term service user:

- It means that we are in an unequal and oppressive relationship with the state and society.
- It is about entitlement to receive welfare services. This includes the past when we might have received them and the present. Some people still need to receive services but are no longer entitled to for many different reasons.
- It may mean having to use services for a long time which separate us from other people and which make people think we are inferior and that there is something wrong with us.
- Being a service user means that we can identify and recognise that we share a lot of experiences with a wide range of other people who use ser-

vices. This might include, for example, young people with experience of being looked after in care, people with learning difficulties, mental health service users, older people, people with physical or sensory impairments, people using palliative care services and people with drug and alcohol problems.
(Shaping Our Lives 2015: 1)

In this sense, McLaughlin (McLaughlin 2009: 1114) proposes to ask the service users themselves what they want to be called. This suggestion must be supported and, as a consequence, the following question arises: To what extent must service users not only participate in the debate of user involvement, but also take an active role in the debate? Beresford and Carr (2012: 33) point out new possibilities for service users to develop their own initiatives and campaigns via social media. There is, for instance, the influential "Spartacus Report" (Dhani/Winyard 2012) in Britain, which was researched, written and published by disabled people and other service users collaborating via social media. (Marsh 2014).

Empowerment

The concept of empowerment is used in different fields and is a discussion topic of controversy in both German and English-speaking countries. A systematic and reflected overview of this concept in the field of social work is presented by Askheim (2003) in English and by Herriger (2014) in German. The following outline of the concept of empowerment is based on both authors.

Two lines of tradition can be identified: One line of tradition is the political participation of all citizens and it is based on the self-help movement, where socially excluded people started to organise themselves. In the United States, they obtained more social and political power at the beginning of 1900 and later in Europe as well (cf. Herriger 2014: 21ff.) The other line of tradition is based on an action programme of professional social work. This line of tradition supports processes of self-organisation and empowerment by service users. It offers resources to implement this type of self-organisation (Herriger 2014: 19; Askheim 2003: 231f.). Here, the understanding of social work turns away from an insufficiently orientated perspective of the service user and points to human strengths instead of weaknesses (ibid.: 64-71). In this context, Herriger has defined empowerment as "a process of development (...) in which people gain strength, which they need for living a better life based on their own standards." (Herriger 2014: 13; own translation). In a similar way, Askheim formulates a "basic understanding" of empowerment because it is difficult to find an adequate definition: "The power should be given to or taken back by those disempowered." (Askheim 2003: 230).

The main and common critical point of the empowerment concept (Herriger 2014: 80-85) is that the self-organisation of life is idealistic: It is problematic to empower people to assume more responsibility and to shape their own life when the conditions of social and political inequality and exclusion remain unchanged. Secondly, the empowerment concept is an excessive demand for independence: It has an understanding of a person without limits, who is stable, perfect and independent without weaknesses. Thirdly, a neoliberal interest is hidden behind the empowerment concept, namely an instrumentalisation of the service user who is supposed to find paid employment as soon as possible.

Furthermore, it is necessary to distinguish the practice of empowerment related to an individual, a collective, or on an institutional or community level (Herriger 2014: 86ff.). The focus on the individual level lies primarily on a psychological empowerment concerning a personal change, e.g. for developing mental and psychological competence. On a community or institutional level, it implies a structural change together with political empowerment, e.g. a street demonstration for a common political interest. Regarding the implementation of the concept of empowerment in the practice of social work, there are several challenges (Herriger 2014: 213ff.).

First, there is a challenge for the professional identity of the individual social worker. For example, there will be no standardised outcomes anymore and success has to be reformulated, because it is different for every user. Alternatively, a collegial understanding of social work has to be developed. Secondly, the relationship between social worker and user can be a challenge in the following situations: when the user refuses to receive empowerment, when the user's wishes are unrealistic (e.g. financially), when there is a need for social protection and control. Thirdly, there are institutional challenges. Social workers have to take account of certain financial and economical boundaries set by their institutional mandate, which limits their perspectives and possibilities. It is also difficult to change a common and widely approved routine. In a similar way, Askheim defines systematically what the concept of empowerment demands from both service users and social workers. There will be negative consequences if these challenges are not successfully resolved (Askheim 2003: 232-237). The implementation of empowerment concepts in the practice of social work can be appropriately "described as a balancing act on a slack rope" for the professional social worker and the service user who have to face these challenges (Askheim 2003: 237). Both Askheim and Herriger affirm that these challenges have to be accepted if a professional empowerment practice is to be applied.

Evaluation

It is very important for the development of projects and courses with user involvement in practice, research and education to be evaluated. However, in general, these evaluations are inadequate and not well known. Schön conducted a systematic analysis of articles in academic journals about user involvement (Schön 2016). She stresses the lack of knowledge about the effects of projects with service user involvement: "projects of user involvement in social work practice are often developed on an ad hoc and inconsistent basis, and knowledge about the effects of these efforts is still limited" (Schön 2016: 31). Further, she detected that service users and social workers describe projects with a gap-mending approach in a positive way. However, there is a "lack of evidence based knowledge" (ibid.). In order to eradicate this flaw, it is important to answer the following crucial questions (Schön 2016: 31):

- How should one proceed with these efforts?
- Which methods produce the most favourable outcomes?
- What does it mean to be in a user role? Is it a stigma or an improvement?
- How does this enhanced knowledge affect students' work and attitudes once they become social workers?

Further, Schön summarizes three very useful categories for evaluating user involvement in social work, education and practice (Schön 2016: 31):

- outcome-focused research on methods and levels of user participation
- users' perceptions of the quality of these activities
- the effect of these activities on a user's quality of life.

There are several evaluations of user involvement in social work education that address the categories given by Schön:

As mentioned at the beginning of this chapter, service user involvement in education has been a mandatory requirement in Britain since 2003. At that time, a new British degree in social work was introduced at the Anglia Ruskin University. Service users and carers[4] are consultants in the education of social work. This means that they are present in class, in the admission process of students or during assessments in social work. For the new implementation of this social work degree, an evidence-based evaluation (Anghel/Ramon 2009) was designed as a research project from 2003-2005. This long-term evaluation included service users, carers, members of the project advisory group (PAG), academic staff, students and internship instructors.

In a long-term study, Robinson and Webber (2013) also evaluated user involvement in social-work education. Students of social work and service users with intellectual impairments participated in this study.

Furthermore, there are some studies which analyse user involvement courses in social work education with a gap-mending approach, e.g. at the Lund University in Sweden, where the first courses started in 2005. Since then, 17 courses have taken place and all the courses were evaluated. The main results were published in an overview (Denvall et al. 2008; Kjellberg/French 2011).

Also, there is a published evaluation of a course at Lillehammer University College in Norway, which includes feedback from students (Askheim 2012).

It is not an easy task to find published evaluations of courses of social work with a gap-mending approach published in English or in other languages. However, this book presents several evaluations of courses within one volume, which include a majority of the mentioned categories of evaluation.

References

Anghel, Roxana; Ramon, Shula (2009): Service users and carers' involvement in social work education: lessons from an English case study. In: *European Journal of Social Work* 12 (2), pp. 185-199.
Askheim, Ole Petter (2003): Empowerment as guidance for professional social work: an act of balancing on a slack rope. In: *European Journal of Social Work* 6 (3), pp. 229-240.

---

4 In the UK, it is common that family members or friends provide unpaid support to related persons (cf. Chapter 3.3).

Askheim, Ole Petter (2012): 'Meeting Face to Face Creates New Insights': Recruiting Persons with User Experiences as Students in an Educational Programme in Social Work. In: *Social Work Education* 31 (5), pp. 557-569.
Beresford, Peter (2005): 'Service user': regressive or liberatory terminology? In: *Disability & Society* 20 (4), pp. 469-477.
Beresford, Peter (2013): From 'other' to involved: user involvement in research: an emerging paradigm. In: *Nordic Social Work Research* 3 (2), pp. 139-148.
Beresford, Peter; Carr, Sarah (Hg.) (2012): Social care, service users and user involvement. London: Jessica Kingsley Publishers (Research highlights in social work, 55).
Beresford, P., and Boxall, K. (2012): 'Service Users, Social Work Education and Knowledge for Social Work Practice'. In: *Social Work Education*, 31/2, pp. 155-167.
Cossar, J.; Neil, E. (2015): Service User Involvement in Social Work Research: Learning from an Adoption Research Project. In: *British Journal of Social Work* 45 (1), pp. 225-240.
Denvall, Verner; Heule, Cecilia; Kristiansen, Arne (2008): Taking the next step – service users and the training of social work students. Lund University. Lund. Retrieved on 29.12.2015 from: http://powerus.se/wp-content/uploads/Taking-the-next-step.pdf.
Dewe, B. (2009): Reflexive Sozialarbeit im Spannungsfeld von evidenzbasierter Praxis und demokratischer Rationalität [Reflective Social Work Between Evidence-Based Practice and Democratic Rationality]. In: Roland Becker-Lenz, S. Busse, G. Ehlert/S. Müller (Hg.): *Professionalität in der sozialen Arbeit. Standpunkte, Kontroversen, Perspektiven [Professionalism in Social Work. Standpoints, Controversies, Perspectives]*. 2. Aufl. Wiesbaden: VS-Verlag für Sozialwissenschaften, pp. 89-109.
Dewe, B.; Otto, H.-U. (2012): Reflexive Sozialpädagogik. Grundstrukturen eines neuen Typus dienstleistungsorientierte Professionshandeln [Reflective Social Work. Basic Structures of a New Type of Service-Oriented Professional Action]. In: Werner Thole (Hg.): *Grundriss Soziale Arbeit. Ein einführendes Handbuch [Outlining Social Work. An Introductory Manual]*. 4. Aufl. Wiesbaden: VS Verlag für Sozialwissenschaften, pp. 197-213.
Dewe, Bernd; Otto, Hans-Uwe (1996): *Zugänge zur Sozialpädagogik. Reflexive Wissenschaftstheorie und kognitive Identität [Social Work Approaches. A Reflective Scientific Theory and Cognitive Identity]*. Weinheim etc: Juventa Verlag.
Directorate General for Employment, Social Affairs and Equal Opportunities of the European Commission (2010): '*Common Quality Framework for Social Services of General Interest*'. Prometheus. Retrieved on 21.01.2016 from: http://www.epr.eu/images/EPR/documents/projects/prometheus/CQF%20for%20SSGI%20-%20FINAL%20VERSION.pdf.
Dhani, Jaspal; Winyard, Steve (2012): Disabled unity. Letter. In: *The Guardian, 20 January* 2012. Retrieved on 13.01.2016 from: http://www.theguardian.com/society/2012/jan/19/disabled-unity-hardest-hit.

Fook, J. (2002): Theorizing from Practice: Towards an Inclusive Approach for Social Work Research. In: *Qualitative Social Work* 1 (1), pp. 79-95.

Fook, Jan (2012): Social work. A critical approach to practice. 2nd edition. Los Angeles: Sage.

Forbes, J.; Sashidharan, S. P. (1997): User Involvement in Services – Incorporation or Challenge? In: *The British Journal of Social Work* 27 (4), pp. 481-598.

Herriger, Norbert (2014): *Empowerment in der Sozialen Arbeit. Eine Einführung [Empowerment in Social Work. An Introduction].* Stuttgart: Kohlhammer Verlag.

Kjellberg, Gun; French, Robert (2011): A New Pedagogical Approach for Integrating Social Work Students and Service Users. In: *Social Work Education* 30 (8), pp. 948-963.

Marsh, Sue (2014): There's a better way to support disabled people – listen to us, for starters *The Guardian*, 9 April 2014, pp. 1. Retrieved 13.01.2016 from: http://www.theguardian.com/society/2014/apr/09/better-way-support-disabled-people-benefits-esa.

McLaughlin, H. (2009): What's in a Name: 'Client', 'Patient', 'Customer', 'Consumer', 'Expert by Experience', 'Service User'—What's Next? In: *British Journal of Social Work* 39 (6), pp. 1101-1117.

Robinson, K.; Webber, M. (2013): Models and Effectiveness of Service User and Carer Involvement in Social Work Education: A Literature Review. In: *British Journal of Social Work* 43 (5), pp. 925-944.

Schön, Ulla-Karin (2015): User Involvement in Social Work and Education-A Matter of Participation? In: *Journal of evidence-informed social work*, pp. 1-13.

Schön, Ulla-Karin (2016): User Involvement in Social Work and Education-A Matter of Participation? In: *Journal of evidence-informed social work* 13 (1), pp. 21-33.

Shaping our Lives (2015): Service user, user controlled. Retrieved on 26.12.2015 from: http://www.shapingourlives.org.uk/about/about-sol/definitions#su.

Thiersch, H. (2013): 'AdressatInnen der Sozialen Arbeit' ["Addressees" of Social Work]. In: G. Grasshoff (ed.), *Adressaten, Nutzer, Agency. Akteursbezogene Forschungsperspektiven in der Sozialen Arbeit ["Addressees", Users, Agency. Addressee-Oriented Research Perspectives in Soical Work].* Wiesen: Springer, pp. 17-32.

3. Examples of courses in Europe

3.1 Sweden: Power, Experiences and Mutual Development. Using The Concept of Gap-Mending in Social Work Education

Arne Kristiansen and Cecilia Heule

What is gap-mending about?

The purpose of this chapter is to give a background to the concept of gap-mending and a description of how we apply it on a course in Social Work at the School of Social Work at Lund University in Sweden. The course, which is called the Mobilisation course, started in 2005. We, the authors of this chapter, have been active as teachers on the course since its inception.

Gap-mending is a concept, which is used to create reflection and analysis of gaps that exist between actors in social work. The gaps we are focusing on are explicit or implicit distinctions between individuals, groups or organisations that are connected in Social Work. It can involve gaps, which are obvious and sometimes even open conflicts, but also cultural assumptions that can seem free from contradictions. Common to the gaps is that they contribute to injustice, subordination and exclusion in social work and society. The gaps inhibit, or sometimes even paralyze, activities in social work to contribute to the positive development of their target groups. The power structures are important grounds for the emergence of the gaps, which are prevailing in society. Power relations between social workers and service users, or between welfare organisations and service user organisations enforce the gaps. According to Foucault, the concept of power, including learning and knowledge, creates control over how people think (1987, 2002). It has an impact on a relational level by influencing people's concrete actions. An important cornerstone in the gap-mending concept is to create awareness of how power relationships and power structures create class differences, exclusion, discrimination and segregation, but also about how the redistribution of power can improve community and social work.

Redistribution of power is central in Hasenfeld's (1992) discussion about power in the social work practice.

> "It is argued that, in most instances, the effectiveness of social work practice is predicated on the enhancement of the power resources of the client" (Hasenfeld 1992: 259).

According to Hasenfeld (1992), the understanding of powers denotation to social work practice is generally underestimated. He describes how different types of power that social workers and their organisations possess have a negative impact on social work practice. Hasenfeld points out how this is reflected in the practical social work, for instance by its focus on the individual and on the problems of service users. In this system the social worker is regarded as an expert of the client's problems. Furthermore the organisation's requirements and interests limit the social worker's discretion. But the main power factor, according to Hasenfeld, is the resources and services that social workers' organisations control and that the organisation's service users are in need of. He argues that social work must change strategy from being problem and individual centred to strategies which gives the service users power over their lives.

> "The essence of these strategies is to create a balance of power between social service agencies and clients. These strategies call for redefining the role of the social worker, harnessing agency resources on behalf of clients, and, most important, reorganizing social service agencies." (Hasenfeld 1992: 273)

The gap-mending concept is not a specific model or method, but should be seen as an analytical approach that can be used in contexts where people meet in common efforts to resolve problems and prevent gaps. The analysis should highlight both problems and opportunities and illustrate power relationships. It can enable mutual learning and development, which contributes to awareness, and changes of the binary and unequal roles which social workers and service users are maintaining in social work practice. It requires that people's needs are given priority and that both service users' experiences and knowledge are considered as valuable and necessary in order to improve society. This also requires that the social workers abandon the role of experts and that the service users abandon the client role. We argue that relationships are crucial for successful social work (Frank/Frank 1991; Wampold 2001, 2010), therefore social work education and practical social work must provide opportunities for relationship-building processes between the people who are actors in social work.

Service User Involvement in Social Work Practice and Social Work Education in Sweden

Nowadays, the importance of the service users' perspective is discussed more frequently in practical social work and in social work education in Sweden. The National Board of Health and Welfare[5] has during many years tried to influence the social services to take greater account to the service users' perspective. One important reason for this is that the National Board of Health and Welfare wants to influence social services to develop an evidence-based practice, which includes taking the service users' perspective into account (Sackett et al. 1997).

Although there is no legislation in Sweden that regulate service user influence in municipal social services, but The National Board of Health and Welfare has issued several publications to provide the municipalities advice and guidance to develop service user participation in their activities (Socialstyrelsen 2003, 2005, 2011, 2013). Nowadays many municipalities in Sweden have service user councils.

When it comes to social work educations in Sweden, the importance of service users' perspectives was pointed out in 2009 in an evaluation made by the Swedish National Agency for Higher Education (Högskoleverket 2009). Today all Swedish social work education at university level has at least one course that highlights a service user perspective.

In recent years some service user groups in Sweden have had an increased influence in relation to social services and to other public authorities. This especially applies to people in the care of elderly people and people with physical or mental disabilities. The development of service user influence has not been as positive for all user groups. When it comes to people with drug problems, poor people or people suffering from mental illness, the case has rather been that social work has become more paternalistic and less user-oriented focus, than the situation a few decades ago (Kristiansen 2009; Heule/Kristiansen 2011). In a study about service user councils in the areas of addiction treatment, care of elderly people and people with physical or mental disabilities in 33 municipalities in southern Sweden, it appeared that the service user councils mainly had an advisory function and rarely affected decisions about care and support interventions (Johansson/Scaramuzzino 2011). Eriksson (2015), who stud-

---

5   The National Board of Health and Welfare (Socialstyrelsen) is a government agency in Sweden under the Ministry of Health and Social Affairs.

ied two different service user participation projects in Sweden, one in psychiatric care and one in municipal social services, shows that the activities of the projects above all concerned procedural issues, in other words how service user influence should be organised, but it had no impact on decisions about support and care interventions should be designed.

The development of user influence in the practical social work in Sweden is also discouraged by the lack of resources in the municipal social services. In many municipalities, the social services are discussed as being in crisis. The Union for Professionals (Akademikerförbundet SSR), a Swedish trade union that organises social workers who are university graduates, has investigated the work situation for social workers in several municipalities. A large section of the social workers have a highly pressurised work situation, which makes it difficult to develop cooperation and good relationships with customers. For example, in the city of Malmö a large number of the social workers reported that their workload is too heavy and that they have difficulty maintaining quality and legal certainty in their work. The survey also shows that the choice of care and support is not guided by the service users' needs, but by the municipality's budget (Akademikerförbundet SSR 2015a, 2015b).

When it comes to the social work educations on university level in Sweden most of them has at least one course focusing on the perspectives of service users, as we mentioned earlier. Our impression is that these courses are often fairly conventional university courses where the emphasis is on teaching about various service user groups. They often include elements whereby people representing different service user interests give lectures about their life experiences, or that students make study visits to service users and their organisations. It is rare that these courses are geared towards gap-mending, which requires a deeper and more long lasting cooperation between teachers, students and people who represent different service user interests. Of course it is positive that social work educations give courses about service user issues, but we wish that more social work educations dared to take a step further, and challenge the traditional teaching methods. Rather than using the service users and their organisations as examples in teaching, they should be related to as partners in the education. Based on our own experiences from the conventional courses in social work where people representing various service user interests have been invited to have lectures about their life experiences, we know that students usually appreciate these elements in the courses and consider them very instructive. But we also know that, even though the intention is to communicate a user's perspective, there is a problem about this type of course structure; namely that it rarely allows a critical analysis of the societal perceptions about service users and social workers, which usually understand the service user as a person with problems and the social worker as an expert on the service users' problems. Instead, there is a risk that such stereotypes and categorisations will be preserved. Social work education, as well as other organisations that work with service user issues, must always ask themselves whether what they do will challenge or can implicate a risk to strengthen the stereotypes linked to the social image of "service users" and "social workers".

Although most of social work education on university level in Sweden today has courses about service user issues, it is obvious that the type of experience-based knowledge, which the service user perspective represents, is essentially subordinated in relation to the knowledge perspectives as research and professional social work represents. A risk with this is that the students will distance themselves from the people they should assist in social work during the education. This concerns a classic problem in medical and paramedical education as well as in social work education, namely that students' empathy in relation to patients and service users tend to deteriorate during their studies. One of the most famous studies of this problem is Boys in White (Becker 1961), a study about medical students in the United States. Holm (2001, 2009), who has studied the same subject, notes that the education programme design is of great importance to the development of the students' empathy. Therefore, medical and social work education can not only be based on theoretical knowledge, but must also contain elements that affect the students emotionally, for example, by meetings face to face with people representing service users interests so that opportunities are given to reflect on these meetings.

The Mobilisation Course at Lund University

Background and pedagogical framework

Since autumn 2005, the School of Social Work at Lund University has given a social work course where social work students and people from different service user organisations study together. The course is titled the Mobilising course and started as an attempt to develop the service user perspective in social work education. When we started the Mobilisation course we had previously used conventional teaching methods to give students knowledge about the importance of service user involvement in social work. For example, we had invited representatives from various service user organisations as guest lecturers and arranged study visits at service user organisations. The students often appreciated these courses, but we felt that this course outline was not sufficient to deepen and touch the students' understanding of the service user's perspective and service user involvement. Later the School of Social Work at Lund University was partnered with the social enterprise Basta in a project funded by the European Social Fund, we got the opportunity within that project to start developing the Mobilisation course.

Pedagogically the Mobilisation course is inspired by alternative teaching methods, which assume that learning and development are an active social process that requires action, interaction and reflection and facilitated by that the students are involved and have influence over the education (Freire 1993; hooks 1994).

There must be an ongoing recognition that everyone influences the classroom dynamic, that everyone contributes. These contributions are resources. Used constructively they enhance the capacity of any class to create an open learning community (hooks 1994: 8).

Our educational goal is to transcend the deficiency and problem oriented approach, which dominates in social work (Kristiansen 1999, 2005; Heule/Kristiansen 2013a). We want to show that the people, who are subject to various interventions in social work, as well as their organisations, are important forces for the development of social work. We want to problematize and transcend the dominant roles and categories in social work in order to create new opportunities for social criticism and for cooperation between service users and social workers. Through the Mobilising course, which is based on the concept of gap-mending, we want to provide students from user organisations and university student's opportunities to study together on equal terms as much as possible.

Our way of applying the gap-mending concept in the Mobilisation course is based on the creation of a joint learning platform, where people who have previously been in different positions of power, together develop new knowledge. Experience-based knowledge is upgraded as an important complement to research and social workers' practice-based experiences. That is the reason why we spend so much time in the initial weeks of the course on personal presentations. The personal presentations are also important for trusting relationships to emerge between students and teachers, which is an important basis for learning and development.

There are three ways of becoming a student on the Mobilisation course. One way is to take it as part of an eligible 15 ECTS-credits course in social work at advanced level in the seventh and last semester on the social work programme. It is also possible to go to a Mobilisation course as part of a 15 ECTS-credits course in social work on the master's programme at the Faculty of Social Sciences at Lund University. For students from the service user organisations, the Mobilising course is a six-week commissioned education in social work at basic level, which gives 7.5 ECTS-credits. It is important to emphasise that the various entrances to the Mobilisation course raise a question about the formal and administrative aspects of the course. In practice it is a coherent course with the same content, and in principle, the same requirements for all students. The only difference is that we must formulate the final individual examination assignments slightly differently depending on whether the student has completed the Mobilisation course at the basic level or advanced level. The system with Commissioned Educations is an opportunity for Swedish universities and colleges to offer governments and company's qualified training for their employees. Commissioned education gives those who are studying on the courses university credits, and makes it possible to make exceptions from admission requirements, which are applicable to ordinary courses on universities and colleges (Molander 2003). The possibility to make exceptions from the admission requirements and to give university credits is important for the Mobilisation course. Although the students who come from the service user organisations have different educational backgrounds, a large majority of them lack formal qualifications to study at the university. In other words, most of them belong to a group in society that are excluded from the possibility of university studies. On a personal level, it can be very meaningful for people who previously barely dreamed of studying at a university to join a course and get university credits. We have had many students' from service user organisations who proudly have told us that they are the first in their family to study at the university and to obtain university credits.

Figure 1. Three ways to attend the Mobilisation Course at the School of Social Work at Lund University in Sweden.

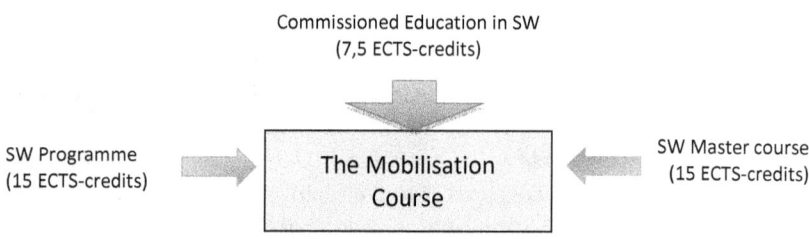

The social work students get information about the Mobilisation course through the School of Social Work via presentations and via the university website. When it comes to the recruitment of students from service user organisations, the responsible teachers have to devote time for personal contacts each semester. In the first years, we spent quite a lot of time communicating and anchoring the vision of the Mobilisation course in different service user organisations. Over time, the Mobilisation course has become better known. Students who have attended the course tell their friends and colleagues about it. Some students hear about the course because of media attention it has received. We still have to devote some time to the recruitment of students, but it has become more common that individuals from service user organisations initiate contact by themselves. Facebook and other forms of social media are also important resources to give information about and promote the Mobilisation course.

Course outline and the pedagogy in practice

Theoretically the course is based on issues about power, inclusion, exclusion, social mobilisation and social change. We try to integrate our vision of cross-boundary community in theory, in the course structure, and in the development of new practice. Research-based knowledge is as valued as service users' knowledge and knowledge from the social practice. Working with the concept of gap-mending in a university environment also requires teachers who are committed and who become involved in the common learning processes. We cannot demand of our students to take risks and challenge themselves if we are not also ready to do it ourselves.

The first day on the course is devoted to information on the schedule, textbooks, etc. The students also do group work, which is a form of a getting to-know-each-other-exercise. Through different exercises they briefly introduce themselves to each other and find out what thing they have in common. We use the format of the independent user-controlled organisation "Shapting Our Lives" and text their text "Suggested Ground Rules for Meetings" (Branfield/Beresford 2010) to discuss the ethical and social framework that will apply for the course. In this discussion we emphasise the importance of listening to each other, and to giving everyone space to express him or herself. It is important to make clear that if someone shares sensitive and personal experiences that it should not be spoken of outside the group. If a student for instance takes pictures, to put out on Facebook or Instagram, those that are photographed must be asked whether they think it's okay. In the coming two weeks the time is devoted to personal presentations, lectures and group work. The lectures and group work are about power, discrimination, social mobilisation, project development and social change. But we also invite people who have built up service user organisations and social enterprises to lecture about their experiences and activities. During the lectures, there are a lot of spontaneous questions from the students, especially students from service user organisations. During group work opportunities are provided for the students to reflect upon questions that are raised during the lectures.

At the end of the second week the students and the teachers have a two-day residential workshop in a small village around 70 km from Lund. We are using a model called Future Workshop (Jungk/Müllert 1987) to develop innovative and alternative project ideas, in order to challenge discrimination, existing power structures and to improve social work practice. During the Future workshop the students forms cross-boundary working groups, which are based on a problem of their interest, which they consider important to change. These working groups will be the basis of the project development, which is occupying a bigger part of the rest of the course. During the project development, students get supervision from the teachers of the course.

In the fifth week their project plans are presented to an external expert panel that provides feedback. The day the working groups present their project plans is a highlight on the course. The students have worked hard together with their project ideas, which they are very interested in and dedicated to. They know they will get relevant and critical comments from the panel, which made up of knowledgeable people who possess leadership positions and have extensive experience working with and evaluating projects. We try to have a breadth in the panel of persons representing different interests in society. Usually we invite a politician, a researcher in social work, a representative of social services and a person who works in a user-led organisation. We do this as a public event, and each semester, for example, former students, people who are interested in attending the course in the future, friends, colleagues and relatives come to listen to the students' presentations. One reason that we have a panel of external people is that we, the teachers of the course tutor working groups while they develop their project plans. A risk with that is that we get too involved and may not see problems and opportunities linked to the project ideas. The project panel has no such ties to the students and their project plans, and can therefore be more open and distanced in their comments. The day after the students present their project plans, we follow up and go through the comments the students received from the panel. It is important to note that it is not the project panel that examines the project plans. It is we who are teachers on the course that determine whether a project plan is approved. In our assessment we assume not only the relevance of the project or how the project panel has received it, but we will also consider such as how students have been involved and active in the project development.

In the last week of the course, the students work with an individual exam question. The task in the exam question is a personal reflection about learning outcomes from interaction with the other students, which must include reflection on the course literature. The students' final reflections are discussed in a seminar. Finally, the Mobilisation course is ended with a joint course evaluation and some ceremonial festivities.

Figure 2. Course outline of the Mobilisation Course at the School of Social Work at Lund University in Sweden.

Week 1	Week 2		Week 3	Week 4	Week 5	Week 6
Personal presentations Lectures Group work	Personal presentations Lectures Group work	FUTURE WORK SHOP	Project Development	Project Development	Project Development Presentation of Project Plans	Examination Course Evaluation

An important goal of the Mobilising course is, as we mentioned above, to provide students from service user organisations and social work students opportunities to study together on as equal terms as possible (Heule/ Kristiansen 2013b). Due to the students' varying backgrounds, this is naturally a challenge. During the past ten years, we have developed an approach that facilitates the platform of mutual and equal development of new knowledge. A fundamental part of this approach is that we try to respond to and treat all students equally regardless of whether they come to the Mobilisation course through the social work programme, the master programme or take the course as a commissioned education. We impose the same requirements for all students in terms of, for example, attendance and participation in various activities. Therefore, we do not use the terms "service user students" and "social work students," but we simply call them students (Heule/Kristiansen 2013a). They're on the Mobilisation course to participate as students in a joint course and everyone's experiences are important, regardless of background. It is very important that we as teachers are aware of and pay attention to this, to avoid contributing to stigmatisation and to maintaining problems linked to certain categorisations or concepts. Sometimes we have to remind each other, our colleagues and students to be consistent in this. The ambition is to – together with the students – problematize and transcend the unequal roles and power relations that exist in social work and which students often carry with them into the Mobilisation course. This reflective activity is a crucial point of departure in the practice of gap-mending, and makes it possible for people and groups to meet, cooperate and develop community and solidarity together. This is shown in the citation below, quoted from a final reflection of a social work student:

> The course started by giving every student the opportunity to share about our selves in front of the whole class. My first thoughts was that this would be a piece of cake, and that I wouldn't have to prepare much. I was going to talk about my recent jobs, and university courses I had taken. But after the first day I had to reconsider. One open hearted presentation after the other had been given. They didn't consist of mechanical recollections about merits, but of unique life experiences. If I had done the presentation that I first had in mind, I would probably have appeared very flat and shallow. I had to start all over. I knew that I would have to make certain adjustments in the course, but was unprepared that it would happen in this way. I had expected that the students from service user organisations would be bitter about their experiences, and eager to regain power. I was surprised when I noticed that many of them chose to be very personal, often being very humorous in spite of – sometimes

> – tragic subjects. /.../ I was moved, and completely changed the planning of my presentation. Suddenly I was hit by performance anxiety, and sat up late one night with a pen and a notebook, sketching what to share. My respect for the fellow students grew as their life stories and personalities took form. I realised that I wouldn't have to be so anxious about the way I related to the students from the service user organisations. They wanted honesty, if possible with humour – not oversensitivity. /.../ A woman in my group said that she was impressed by my presentation. It felt great, in spite of that her life had been so much more dramatic. I had been moved by her story. (Social work student)

As the citation clearly communicates, the narrative of fellow students affects the students personally, and it changes the way they look at themselves. The personal presentations constitute an important strategy to challenge and transcend various stereotypical roles that upholds prejudices and inequality. The social work students express that it's a relief to be able to consider their personal history and take it into account in developing a professional role in social work practice. They also express that the narratives of the service users impress them. The service users are not used to being honest and equal when meeting representatives of professional social work, and find it empowering to be able to share from an equal platform. One of the service user students expressed this in his final exam:

> Before the course started I had certain fears. What, and how much would I tell about myself and about my life? Early in the course, every participant should make a personal presentation, telling our classmates about who we were. During this time, it became clear that social work students had experienced different social problems themselves. I experienced that this tore down barriers. My background is that of a heroin addict, and I have been convicted for different self-defence crimes connected to my time as an addict. It is easy to be categorised, and singled-out when you have a specific background. The personal presentations gave me an opportunity to tell the whole picture of who I was and of my history. I am not only what can be read in different journals or crime records. I am so much more than an addict, client, patient and so on. The same goes for the social work students. They are not only their academic exams, or professional titles. They often carry an interesting background that they should make use of in social work practice. I experienced that the social work students, as well as the students from service user organisations, took the presentations very seriously./.../ My experience is that many of us service users self censure ourselves when meeting professional social workers. They hold the power of our cases and in the end of our lives. It is naturally sensitive to discuss every aspect of ones life with some-

one with the power to write journals, to categorise and to decide over benefits and regulations. In such situations I often remain silent. To pretend to be less intelligent than one is when confronted with people with power over you, is unfortunately not unusual. (Student from service user organisation)

We devote quite a lot of time during the first weeks of the Mobilisation course to these narratives. As the service user expresses in the citation above, it makes the students reflect upon the difference that occur when the relationships are characterized by equality and curiosity, rather than distance and categorisation. During the personal presentations, each student gets about 15 minutes to tell the class about himself or herself and what matters to them within social work practice. Every semester the students are surprised and concerned by what they are told by their classmates. We take part in stories about experiences of vulnerability and experience of being beneficiaries of social services, as well as stories about happiness and success. The personal presentations make it possible for the students to build relationships that are crucial for their cooperation and mutual development. Based on Wenger (1998), the personal presentations can be regarded as stories in a communicative practice, which creates a repertoire of shared experiences, contributing to better cooperation and trust between the students.

What has come out of the Mobilisation Course?

Since autumn 2005 we have carried out the Mobilisation course 18 times, with a total of 626 students completing it. 205 of the students have taken the course as a commissioned course, 398 students have taken it as part of the social work programme, and 23 students have been master's students. Table 1 shows that there are gender differences between the different student groups. There are also age differences. The students who access the Mobilisation course via commissioned education have a higher average age than the students who access the Mobilisation course through the social work programme and the master's programme. The students who have done the Mobilisation course as part of a commissioned education represent about fifty different service user organisations. We have tried ensuring as broad a variety as possible in terms of service user organisations that we cooperate with. Today we have cooperation with organisations that are run by a variety of service user groups, such as substance abuse, mental illness, homelessness, disabilities and ethnic minorities.

Table 1. Number of students on the Mobilisation Course at the School of Social Work at Lund University in Sweden.

Students		Female	Male
Commissioned Education	205	88	117
Social work programme	398	328	70
Social work master course	23	15	8
Total	626	431	195

We evaluate the Mobilisation course in different ways. In the end of every course the students answer a course questionnaire. We also have frequent discussions during the course with the students about what happens in the course and how they experience it. Most importantly, as the basis for our evaluation and development work is the individual reflections which the students write at the end of each course. Although many argue that it is a demanding course, so are the vast majority of students very happy and excited that they have chosen to take the course. Many of the students who take the course as part of the social work programme mean that it has been the most instructive and important course throughout the social work programme and that it should be mandatory for all social work students.

Impact and dissemination

The Mobilisation course, which started ten years ago as a pilot project of service user inclusion in social work education, is today an established part of the elective courses at the School of Social Work at Lund University. As we mentioned earlier, more than 600 students have passed the Mobilisation course. Over 200 of the students come from different service user organisations. Many of those have later been involved in other courses of the Social Work programme at Lund University as guest lecturers and tutors. Through the students who have attended the course as a Commissioned Education, we have built up a network of over fifty different user organisations, covering a range of areas related to social work.

The Mobilisation course can be described as a gap-mending, action research-oriented platform for networking, development of innovative and alternative solutions to social problems and research. Those teaching the course are often asked to participate in various conferences and debates concerning service user participation and development of alternative solutions to social problems in Sweden, and abroad. Through the years we have participated in a number of conferences and seminars on service user involvement in other universities, municipalities and in other types of organisations. Several of the project ideas developed during the Mobilisation course have been realized in different contexts. Some new service user organisations have been developed based on ideas from, and networks around the Mobilising course. One example is the G7 in Helsingborg, which is a peer support organisation for people who are or have been homeless. Another example is a self-help organisation for parents of children who are or have been placed in foster care (Maskrosforaldrar 2016). Many of our former students are active in development projects in various organisations and municipalities in Sweden. One example was when the city of Malmö started a project to develop the service user perspective in their social services a few years ago. A large number of the service users who participated in the project were former students of the Mobilisation course. Another example is when the county of Scania in the south of Sweden, conducted a project to develop service user involvement in mental health services. In the same way, many of the representatives from service user organisations had participated in the course.

The Mobilisation course has been a vital partner in the development of the international network PowerUs. The courses integrating social work students and students from service user organisations were first developed in Lund, Sweden, and have been followed by similar courses in other countries from the PowerUs network.

References

Akademikerförbundet SSR (2015a): *Krisen i socialtjänsten måste vändas nu* [The crisis in the social services must be reversed now]. Stockholm: Akademikerförbundet SSR (https://akademssr.se/reportage/krisen-i-socialtjansten-maste-vandas-nu) Cited 160105.

Akademikerförbundet SSR (2015b): *Kartläggning socialsekreterare Malmö stad* [Survey Social workers City of Malmo]. Stockholm: Akademikerförbundet SSR (https://akademssr.se/dokument/2015-01-19-novus-kartlaggning-socialsekreterare-malmo-stad) Cited 160105.

Becker, Howard S. (ed.) (1961): *Boys in white: student culture in medical school.* Chicago: University of Chicago Press.

Branfield, Fran/Beresford, Peter (2010): *Count us in! Involving everyone in health and social care research. Report of a service user workshop run by Shaping Our Lives for INVOLVE.* London: Shaping Our Lives.

Eriksson, Erik (2015): *Sanktionerat motstånd brukarinflytande som fenomen och praktik* [Sanctioned resistance: Service user involvement as phenomenon and practice]. Lund: Socialhögskolan, Lunds universitet.

Foucault, Michel (1987): *Övervakning och straff: fängelsets födelse* [Discipline and Punish. The Birth of the Prison]. Lund: Arkiv förlag.

Foucault, Michel (2002) *Vetandets arkeologi* [The Archaeology of Knowledge]. Lund: Arkiv förlag.

Frank, Jerome D./Frank, Julia B. (1991): *Persuasion and healing. A comperative study of psychotherapy.* Baltimore: The John Hopkins University Press.

Freire, Paolo (1996): *Pedagogy of the Oppressed.* London: Penguin books.

Hasenfeld, Yeshekel (1992): Power in Social Work Practice. In: Hasenfeld, Yeheskel (red.) *Human services as complex organizations.* London: Sage.

Heule, Cecilia/Arne Kristiansen (2011): "Språk och begrepp som mobiliserande eller stigmatiserande faktorer" [Language and concepts as mobilizing or stigmatizing factors]. In: Denvall, Verner, Cecilia Heule/Arne Kristiansen (red) *Social mobilisering. En utmaning för socialt arbete.* Lund: Gleerups.

Heule, Cecilia/Arne Kristiansen (2013a): Vem är brukare? Kan en brukare representera andra brukare än sig själv? [Who is the service user? Can a service user represent other service users than themselves?]. *Socialpolitik* 2013/1.

Heule, Cecilia/Arne Kristiansen (2013b): *Mend the gap – a teaching method for a mobilising social work.* Lund: School of Social Work, Lund University.

Holm, Ulla (2009): *Det räcker inte att vara snäll: Förhållningssätt, empati och psykologiska strategier hos läkare och andra professionella hjälpare* [It is not enough to be nice: Approach, empathy and psychological strategies of physicians and other professional helpers]. Stockholm: Natur och Kultur.

Holm, Ulla (2001): *Empati: Att förstå andra människors känslor* [Empathy: Understanding other people's emotions]. Stockholm: Natur och Kultur.

hooks, bell (1994): *Teaching to transgress: Education as the Practice of Freedom.* London: Routledge.

Högskoleverket (2009): *Utvärdering av socionomutbildningen vid svenska universitet och högskolor* [Evaluation of the social work education at Swedish universities and colleges]. Stockholm: Högskoleverket.

Jungk, Robert/Mullert, Norbert (1987): *Future workshops: How to create desirable futures.* London: Institute for Social Inventions.

Kristiansen, Arne (1999): *Fri från narkotika. Om kvinnor och män som har varit narkotikamissbrukare* [Free from drugs. On women and men who have been drug abusers]. Umeå: Studier i socialt arbete nr 28, Institutionen för socialt arbete, Umeå universitet.

Kristiansen, Arne (2005): *Flickor i tvångsvård. Utvärdering av tolvstegsinriktad §12-vård* [Girls in compulsory treatment. Assessment of a twelve step oriented §12-treatment]. Stockholm: Statens institutionsstyrelse.

Kristiansen, Arne (2009): "Ett brukarperspektiv på dagens missbruksvård" [A service user perspective on today's addiction treatment]. In: *Missbruk och behandling. Gamla problem – nya lösningar?* Socialtjänstforum – ett möte mellan forskning och socialtjänst. Göteborg 21–22 april 2009. Forskningsrådet för arbetsliv och socialvetenskap.

Maskrosforaldrar (2016): *Collapsed Parenthood – disqualified Mothers, Lost Fathers and Childrens Right to Their Parents.* (http://www.maskrosforaldrar.se/) Cited: 2016-01-11.

Molander, Barbro (2003): *Uppdragsutbildning – En vägledning: Tillsynsrapport* [Commissioned Education – A Guidance: Inspection Report]. Stockholm: Högskoleverket.

Sacket, David. L./Straus, Sharon E./Richardson, Scott/Rosenberg, William/Haynes, R. Brian (1997): *Evidence Based Medicine: How to Pratice and Use EBM.* New York: Churchill Livingstone.

Socialstyrelsen (2003): *Brukarmedverkan i socialtjänstens kunskapsutveckling* [Service user involvement in social services knowledge development]. Stockholm: Socialstyrelsen.

Socialstyrelsen (2005): *Integration mellan forskning, utbildning och praktik ur ett brukarperspektiv* [Integration between research, education and practice from a service user perspective]. Stockholm: Socialstyrelsen.

Socialstyrelsen (2011): *Metoder för brukarinflytande och brukarmedverkan inom socialtjänst och psykiatri: en kartläggning av forskning och praktik* [Methods for service user participation and service user involvement in social services and psychiatry: a survey of research and practice]. Stockholm: Socialstyrelsen.

Socialstyrelsen (2013): *Att ge ordet och lämna plats: vägledning om brukarinflytande inom socialtjänst, psykiatri och missbruks- och beroendevård* [To give the word and leave space: Guidance on service user influence in social, psychiatric and substance abuse and addiction care]. Stockholm: Socialstyrelsen.

Wampold, Bruce E. (2010): *The basics of psychotherapy: an introduction to theory and practice.* Washington, DC: American Psychological Association.

Wampold, Bruce E. (2001): *The Great Psychotherapy Debate. Models, Methods and Findings.* Mahwah, New Jersey: Lawrence Erlbaum Associates.

Wenger, Etienne (1998): *Communities of practice: Learning, Meaning, and Identity.* Cambridge: Cambridge University Press.

3.2 Norway: Do Gap-Mending Methods Have any Long-Term Effects? Experiences from the Norwegian Course 'Meeting Face to Face Creates Insights'

Liv Altmann, Tove Hasvold and Ole Petter Askheim

Lillehammer University College (LUC) since 2009 has provided the course 'Face to Face Creates Insights', where individuals with experiences as a service user participate as students on equal terms together with the bachelor students in social work, child welfare and social education. Through gap-mending methods, LUC has established a common learning arena that both acknowledges the service users' experiences and considers them essential as a necessary complement to knowledge in the field of social work.

The comments from the participating students upon immediately completing the course have been very positive. However, whether the course has any lasting positive effects on the programmes of study, whether it enhances and changes professional practice, and whether it improves service users' outcomes are the crucial criteria of whether such a course has been successful or not. A comprehensive literature review of projects with service user involvement in social work education has concluded that there is insufficient empirical evidence demonstrating either that service user involvement improves outcomes for students or that it has a favorable effect on social work practice or on outcomes for future service users (Robinson/Webber 2013). On the basis of this review, we have conducted interviews with former students in the spring of 2014 in order to find out whether we could identify any long-term effects this course has had on our students.

In this chapter, we shall first give a brief account of social work and social work education in a Norwegian context. We follow this with a presentation of the course and its ideological and pedagogical foundations. We shall then briefly present the participating students' comments upon the completion of the course before we present and discuss the results from the interviews with the former students in more detail.

Social work and social work education in the Norwegian context

In Norway there are three separate accredited professional studies for social workers: social work, child-welfare work and what is called 'social education', which denotes the services for persons with intellectual impairments. There are 12 institutions offering bachelor courses in social work, 11 in child welfare work, and 12 in social education. A growing number are taking different master's courses relevant to social work. About 26,500 people work as social workers in Norway. Most of them work in the public sector, and, of these, the municipalities employ the majority, in the areas of social services, childcare, rehabilitation and home-based care. Moreover, a significant number are state employees working in hospitals, psychiatric institutions, child-care institutions and so on. A growing number are finding employment with private institutions and non-governmental organizations (NGOs).

Casework is the main feature of social work. Community work has a modest position, and there is a tendency for both preventive work and community work to be given lower priority.

The involvement of users in the social work and social education courses has been minimal. Traditionally people with user experience give guest lectures; otherwise, the students mainly meet them as clients during their mandatory period of practical work experience.

Background for the course

As lecturers at the Faculty of Education and Social Work at Lillehammer University College, we have since 2009 organized a three week course where persons with service user experiences participate on equal terms with bachelor students in social work, child welfare and social education. For the bachelor students the course takes place during the last term of their programme.

The reason for the establishment of the course was the recognition that the social work educational programmes realize the objectives of user involvement only to a very small degree. The aim of the course is to emphasise empowerment and service user involvement in social work. The course represents a new teaching practice in the social work educational programmes. Teachers and students work closely together in partnership with persons with service user experience. The focus is on collaborative learning and recognition of experience-based competence. We named the course 'Meeting Face to Face Creates Insights'. The title underscores our strongly held conviction that it is in the intersection between the experience-based and the professional competence where new insights might develop (Askheim/Altmann/Gardli/Hasvold 2010; Askheim 2012).

Since 2009, the course has been arranged six times. 189 students have participated, 68 of these were externally recruited students, and 121 were students from the bachelor programmes. We considered the ideal number of participants in each course to be 30, 15 internal and 15 external students. However, the number of participants was some years higher and closer to 40. Various service user organisations and treatment facilities were a necessary link in the recruitment of the external students.

The course content

The topics of the course reflect its aim, which is to provide insights into:

- Power and powerlessness in the relation between the service user and the service provider.
- What empowerment means on different levels (individual, group and system levels).
- How user competence and professional competence can complement each other.
- How empowerment can be realised in practice.

These topics closely connect both to individual and collective processes of becoming conscious of the mechanisms of suppression that take place in the encounter between professionals and service users and to the mobilization of counterpower.

During the course, the students work intensely together, four days every week for three weeks. The remaining day of each week is for individual studies. The course begins with a day-to-day seminar located outside the college (it includes staying overnight). In this seminar the students work together using experience-based and creative methods derived from art and expressive therapy (Levine/Levine 1999), which are well suited for promoting community, building trust and creating a safe learning environment. The second part comprises lectures that aim to illuminate the concept of empowerment. Discussion groups composed of students with different backgrounds follow, and the students then participate in plenary sessions. Finally, the students conduct a group project, which they present to everyone. The presentation takes place in a variety of ways, such as role playing or video productions, and has oral and written components. This presentation constitutes the final exam.

The students' immediate responses

On the first day of the course, each student writes down his or her expectations. At the end of the course, the students write about whether their expectations have been met, and they are invited to elaborate on their experiences. The student makes his or her comments anonymously, but we ask every student to mark whether he or she is an external or internal student.

The main impression from these evaluations is that the students are very positive (Askheim/Altmann/Hasvold 2014). All of them, both external and internal students, underline that they have gained an increased understanding of what the concept of empowerment means in theory and practice.

The external students make references to personal development and describe how the course has increased their self-confidence and strength in different ways. Some of them describe it as their 'first good experience with school'. Further, they point to the good feeling of being a part of a community. Many of them express satisfaction, both with the fact that they contribute to future social workers' more nuanced understanding of both who the service user is and what service user competence is about. Others emphasise that they have gained a deeper comprehension both of themselves and of the service support system.

The internal students express that they have developed their understanding of empowerment as an approach, and that their relational competence has been challenged in practice. They have gained new insights and experiences, both in their views of themselves and of the service users. They view their learning experience as beneficial and relevant for their future roles as social workers.

Does service user involvement in education have any long-term effects?

Robinson and Webber (2013) have conducted a literature review where they summarise the effects of service user involvement in social work education. Not only have they tried to determine whether service user involvement influences the participants, but they have also attempted to document any effects on social work practice, any changes in organisational structures, and so forth. They found that only to a limited degree is it possible to document any long-term effects from service user involvement in the education programmes. Their conclusion is that there is little empirical evidence to support that service user perspective and participation affect the students' attitudes and competence in this area. They also claim that no study has documented any effect on social work practice, or have any effects for future service users.

Furthermore, Robinson and Webber (2013) stress that service user involvement in education is insufficient as an aim in itself. User involvement has to be meaningful, and there is a need to define much more specifically what the overarching goals are. They find no agreement in the literature about what constitutes meaningful involvement in higher education, nor for whom. They question if there are some existing contradictions in the understanding of what this kind of involvement really entails. Some will claim that the purpose of user involvement is to improve the quality of social work education, thus enhancing professional practice, and consider this as an aim in itself. Others will solely be concerned with the empowerment of the service users involved, and insist that user involvement only becomes meaningful if it benefits the service users.

Interviews in reflection groups

In order to investigate whether our course had any long-term influence on the service users' situation and for social work practice, we conducted a follow-up study in 2014. The students from the first two courses were the ones most relevant to ask to investigate possible long-term influences. We chose group interview as the methodological approach. We considered this method to be consistent with the sharing of knowledge and the partnership that was added as a premise for the course.

We e-mailed 19 selected students who participated in the course in 2009 or 2010 who we presumed were living within a reasonable distance to LUC. We ended up with a group of nine students (four internal and five external) who agreed to participate in reflection groups connected to the learning outcomes of the course. We arranged three meetings for the reflection groups.

We used a semi-structured interview guide. We determined the topics we wanted to explore beforehand. The structure of the conversation was loose, and we asked open-ended questions about the participants' memories from the course: What, if anything, from the course do they consider to be important today? The conversations proceeded in a relatively relaxed, rather informal manner and the participants themselves kept the discussions going. The former students and teachers followed up different claims and formulations of opinions in order to uncover further details and distinctions. The fixed topics that the teachers wanted to learn more about related to the group members' views on the introductory seminar, the potential to improve the course, and future recommendations.

One of us transcribed the material and noted important statements, and the others also noted what was interesting in the material. We then worked together with the analysis of the material using what Blaikie (1993) calls 'abduction', a combination of induction and deduction where theoretical studies serve as an inspiration for finding patterns and meanings in the data.

The nine students represented a small selection of the total number of participants.

We cannot say if their experiences of learning outcomes are representative for the student group as a whole. Student groups are heterogeneous, and students have different viewpoints when they begin the course. However, in spite of these methodological limitations, the clarity and the consistency of the students' comments indicate the answers having strong validity. We also sent a draft of the analysis to the participants so that they would have the opportunity to read and comment on the text. We took this measure in order to avoid any simplified interpretations, naive recommendations and hasty conclusions. We did not receive any comments to the draft. This could indicate that our analysis is reasonable. Alternatively, the reason for the absence of comments could be connected to the more theoretical and academic nature of the analysis, and may be of limited interest to the group members.

Results

The former students illustrated through stories and reflections how the course has influenced their attitudes, values and actions. We have organised their answers in themes, under the following five headlines:

'experiencing oneself as part of a "we"'
'on categorizing and stigmatization'
'on repression, power, roles and role-changing'
'partnership and loyalty with the oppressed'
'togetherness, emotional energy and self-worth'.

Experiencing oneself as part of a "we"

Both the external and the internal students claimed to have developed a clear awareness of the significance of mutual respect and recognition. They emphasized that important conditions for this were already in place at the introductory seminar. Our goals with the introductory seminar were to facilitate symmetry and equality among the participants by gathering on neutral ground and by working with creative methods.

Several of the participants, especially the internal students, said they had initially been quite skeptical to such methods. They described creative methods as 'not my thing' or 'it can easily become awkward' to partake in these activities.

Several of the students explained how this attitude changed from negative to positive during the opening seminar. The participants positively evaluated the opening seminar upon completion of the course, and in the reflection groups, it became evident that this perception had endured. The balance between fun and seriousness worked:

It challenged me. I had to present myself in ways that I was not comfortable with, and it challenged me and my boundaries. But it did not become awkward; it was very good!

All nine students emphasised that without the introductory seminar, the experiences of proximity, contact and respect would not have been the same.

One of the former internal students argued that the experience of being brought outside your comfort zone is an important and useful experience that can influence future social workers' attitudes and understanding of service users' circumstances and needs later in their practical work.

On categorization and stigmatization

Categorization and stigmatisation involves reductionism. One is reduced to one's stigma, or to a member of a disparaged category. In empowerment theory, such a lack of recognition is referred to as oppression (Freire 1970). Both the internal and the external students expressed an increased awareness of this theme. At the opening seminar we did not introduce the students to each other as being either internal or external students. The participants in the reflection groups described in various ways how this helped to free them from categorizing each other:

We were was much more on the same level, so to say, by not having a category that one belonged to in a way. As if I am a student and I belong in this or that programme and I am from the X institution, you know... I think in relation to power, that if you say that you are in this or that educational programme, then you have already made that distinction; there is this need to place each other in boxes... I think that in itself is counterproductive. If we already at the beginning had created such categories, then there is no service user involvement and no empowerment thinking.

Simply being a fellow student had contributed to external students' increased understanding of others' categorizing and of their own self-oppression. One of the former external students expressed it like this:

How long will I have to be an ex-addict? When will I be just me again?

According to Honneth (1996) lack of recognition can be an expression of contempt. One way of showing someone contempt is to act as if the other was not physically present, as if he or she were invisible. One external student told about her experiences from meetings with what is called in Norway a *'support group'*[6]. At one meeting she argued that the time had come for her to scale down her dosage of methadone. When the physician answered, he addressed his answer to the other professionals in the room. The former external student then interrupted and asked the physician to address his answer to her, since she was the one who had asked the question and the situation was about her. After having pointed this out, the climate of the meeting changed, and the student experienced that she was no longer ignored in the same way. The meetings developed in such a way that the student today sits at the head of the table, leading her own meetings.

This illustrates how the former external student has disclosed oppression and has verbally resisted the helpless and passive role she has been allotted. She now uses her ability to recognize oppression along with a confidence in her own worth; she now authorises herself as a partner. In this way she has been able to resist the passive role, which might have continued otherwise. As Coleridge (1993) claims, 'it is easy to recognise an empowered person' (Coleridge 1993: 53) partly because this person has learned about constructive confrontation.

---

6   A support team dedicated to those with complex need of support, including those in drug treatment comprising both the professionals involved and the service user.

On repression, power, roles and role-changing

During the reflection meetings, it emerged that several of the former external students had strengthened and recognised their own experience-based competence through sharing knowledge with fellow students. This increases self-confidence, and encourages the resistance to injustice. Increased self-confidence and awareness of power and of means of power can promote the necessary changing of experienced oppressive practices.

In the dialogue meetings, the students reflected on oppressive mechanisms.

One of the former internal students said:

I don't relate to the rule that the chair in the office should be raised to a level above the service users, and that the service users are not supposed to have access to the computer screen.

One former external student talked about how the label of 'ex-addict' hinders communication, for instance, with the social services. She gave an illuminative example: when she is rejected too many times at the switchboard of the office, she changes tactics and presents herself as her coordinator, saying that she is calling on her behalf. Here, this former student shows that she is aware of how the switchboard at the social services filters calls, depending on who is calling. She is capable of revealing this use of power, and she applies counterpower.

Partnership and loyalty with the oppressed

Both the former internal as well as the external students stated that they have become more aware of the significance of the others' experiences and competences in all forms of cooperation. They accentuated the value of sharing knowledge and new ways of applying knowledge.

Several of the internal students emphasized that they see the value of co-operating with service users more clearly.

The coordinated collaborative learning with the external students had convinced them that good solutions can only be found in partnership with others.

One of the former internal students expressed the cooperative partnership as follows:

I work together with service users, I don't work with cases.

Former internal students stressed that they have an understanding of partnership as a value-based cooperation that includes a loyalty to the service user. The following statement expresses this view:
I bend the rules for the benefit of those who need it.

The statement suggests that this former internal student's loyalty primarily lies with the service user, not with the system. For this student this value-based foundation was an important reason for participating in the course. She still asserted that the course had been important to her because it has strengthened her foundation of values in her performance of social work. This is how she expressed it:
Empowerment is not just an approach in social work; it is also an integrated part of my professionalism and my personality.

The loyalty and the alliance with the service user are also highlighted in other ways. Another former internal student told how she finds that her colleagues seem to be in conflict with service users to a much greater extent than she is. Another internal student stated that she finds it difficult when the employer imposes tasks and sets short deadlines and by doing so almost dictates how tasks should be solved without consideration of the best interest of the service user. The employer's commands and tasks limit her professional autonomy and her freedom to make her own ethical decisions. Additionally, it leaves little room for the service user to exert influence on his or her own life. The student illustrated this with the following example:

In spite of her protests, her employer went on Christmas holiday with the expectation that the staff on duty would carry out the testing of new patients during the holidays. She then faced the dilemma of whether to follow her employer's instructions and deadlines or to be true to her own value-based convictions and to recognise that patients have the right to have a holiday free of testing. Empowerment and the idea of partnership influenced the former internal student's approach to this problem: decisions should not be taken without involving the service user, and testing cannot be performed without cooperation. Thus, testing was not conducted during the holidays. She perceives that the deadlines and the demands for efficiency are means of power that the employer uses to oppress both her professional and value-based beliefs and her loyalty to the service user. The former internal student thus chose to be loyal to the service users, and protested against the oppressive practices in the institution. She practices what the Swedish researcher

Maria Modig calls 'The Required Disobedience' (Modig 1984, authors' translation).

Community, emotional energy and self-worth

The confidence and the courage that several of the former external students describe as having developed from the course correspond with 'emotional energy', as Starrin (2007) describes it. According to Starrin, emotional energy is closely connected to empowerment, and it is stimulated in situations and relations where we feel that we are accepted and recognized. Starrin emphasizes that emotional energy is experienced as 'enthusiasm, solidarity, self-confidence and vigour' (Starrin 2007: 62, authors' translation).

All of the former external students emphasised that the course had contributed to a meaningful experience of belonging to a community. Several of them emphasised the joy, the good feelings and the energy they experienced by being a student in this community:

Queuing up with all the other students in the cafeteria, to feel like one of the crowd – that was a great feeling!

Coming to the college every day made me feel like all the others.

...after the course, all of us at the institution were 'high' on empowerment.

I could feel it when I walked in the main entrance here at the university college a few minutes ago; there is a special atmosphere here; my heart started beating a little harder....it is an exciting place to be; it definitely does something to me.

These experiences relate to the experiences of community. Being a part of a community, not being one of 'the others', leads to an experience of social recognition. The participants' finding themselves 'high on empowerment' reflects 'emotional energy' (Starrin 2007). Emotional energy is compatible with Honneth's (1996) concept of 'social recognition', which is a special form of recognition that individuals experience on the basis of their participation and engagement in the community:

I gained confidence by developing my ability to express myself. To speak out. I was listened to. This has had an impact on how I perceive who I am today.

This student's statement indicates that she perceived herself as a positive contribution to the community. She stated that the experience of being listened to, being seen and respected had a significant effect on her self-esteem.

The participation in the course also seems to have influenced and changed the external students' self-perception. This might have, as some of them pointed out, initiated some significant changes. Several of the external students expressed a change in their understanding of the possibilities of education. Whereas a college education had earlier seemed to be too far out of reach, it now seemed possible. One of the former external students described how she, after having participated in the course, began collecting the certificates from all her former workplaces as well as diplomas from former schooling. She was now motivated and mobilized for further studies. She had her prior learning assessed – something she had never thought of doing before. Becoming aware that you have the same rights and can qualify for the same education as the internal students promotes experiences of control and power:

I was bitten by the 'school-bug', you know, after having participated in the course.

Two of the external students said that they have now begun higher education. A third related that she has retaken 12 exams. Her aim was to be admitted into a university college.

Concluding reflections

What has emerged from the reflection meetings appears to show that 'gap-mending' methods have benefitted both former internal and external students on a long-term basis. Former internal students claimed that participating in the course had among other things changed their attitudes and perceptions of the social worker's as well as of the service user's role, and as a consequence the orientation of their practice has changed too. The external students described increased awareness about mechanisms of oppression, self-worth and status as equal participants, and how this has affected how they act in the role as service user today. The changes the former students attributed to the participation in the course contrasts with Robinson and Webber's (2013) conclusion in their literature review.

The differences between Robinson and Webber's and our findings can be due to several factors. Their data material is mainly based on service users' participation in admission interviews for studies, service users' assessment of students' assignments and service user lectures. These are measures well suited to clarify and recognise a service user perspective, but they differ from our course, where the internal and external students *learn together*. Our study is based on gap-mending methods that reflect a partnership between the student and the service user, which Robinson and Webber have not studied. In their literature review, Robinson and Webber (2013) discuss how the concept of meaningful can be defined in relation to involvement in higher education. According to Beresford 'meaningful involvement is defined as evidence of change or improvements' (Beresford 2005, in Robinson/Webber 2012: 1258). On the basis of the former internal students' reflections, we believe it is legitimate to claim that participation in the course has been meaningful because they have experienced an increased awareness of social work values and have applied this in practice. In this way it benefits the service users. Another expression of experienced meaningfulness is that all the students emphasised that the course ought to be compulsory for all students.

The immediate responses following the participation of the course also dovetail with what the students had expressed four-five years later. The former students repeated and elaborated on in the reflection meetings what they emphasised as being valuable at the end of the course. Looking back, they were able to point at specific factors they believed could be attributed to the participation in the course. There are indications that the former internal students' professional practice mirrors solid basic values. They pointed out and exemplified how their perspectives on the social worker role had grown after having participated in the course. Solidarity implies regarding the other as a valuable contributor, and is more than just expressing respect and tolerance. It is to recognise that goals are reachable only through cooperation and partnership. The internal students' focus is directed especially to the partnership with service users. They also stated that after completing their studies they have chosen lines of work that encourages practicing empowerment, and that they have actively rejected work where they have experienced an insufficient emphasis on service user involvement, and where power- and rule-based practice is dominant. The external students consistently presented examples that show increased awareness of oppressive mechanisms, self-worth and status as equal partners. The participation in the community had contributed to a deep-felt experience of social recognition. The increased self-worth seems to have mobilised them, both with respect to awareness and power to act against self-oppression and oppression from others.

Future recommendations

We think that user involvement in education is necessary and possible. Our chosen format with a limited number of students in the course is, however, a challenge with respect to that all the students should be offered the course. Nevertheless, it is our viewpoint that 'gap-mending' methods and cooperative learning presuppose a small and manageable group. This is an important condition for making it possible for everybody to be seen and heard. This is essential with regard to the mechanisms we sometimes can observe at the beginning of the course.

There are, of course, shortcomings. We could see that some of the internal students took on a 'professional responsibility' to interact with the external students with a harmonized form of respect that includes 'care, instead of confrontation' or 'the service user is always right'. This means that some of the internal students entered the partnership with the expectations to fill a 'traditional professional supporter role', where the external student is to be taken care of instead of being challenged. This is in reality an underestimation of the external student and a prejudiced assumption that the external students are incapable of receiving criticism, considering comments or broadening their perspectives.

We have also noticed that at times this tendency of the internal students to assign themselves the role of helper leads to some external students to take on the role of someone in need of help. The teachers have to be aware that this dynamic can occur. This presupposes that the teachers are able to spot and disclose these situations and to lead the students back on the right track towards equal participation.

The teachers need good abilities to disclose these situations, and the ability to supervise and facilitate them. If the teachers do not have the ability to see and intervene, the distinction between 'us' and 'them' will solidify, and the prerequisite for shaping an 'us' will remain elusive.

In other words, the teachers have to be able to cover a wider teaching role than is expected in ordinary teaching. We have experienced that the teacher role is characterised as a facilitator, and it requires the theory of recognition and empowerment as a fundamental professional and value-based practice.

The future challenge will be to ensure that all social work students will have the opportunity to experience cooperative learning processes with persons with service user experiences. To achieve this, a channel for sharing knowledge, support and inspiration is needed. The PowerUs network may be an important source of inspiration in this regard. A change of structures presupposes a partnership between allies, and a network like this can be an important tool for promoting cooperation and equality.

References

Altmann, Liv/Hasvold, Tove (2015). Brukerinvolvering i sosialfaglig utdanning. Hva kan «gap-mending» pedagogikk bidra til? [User involvement in social work education: what can 'gap-mending' pedagogics contribute to?] *Fontene Forsking*, 2, pp. 77-89.

Askheim, Ole Petter (2012): 'Meeting Face to Face Creates Insights': Recruiting Persons with User Experiences as Students in an Educational Programme in Social Work. *Social Work Education*, no. 5, pp. 557-569.

Askheim, Ole Petter,/Altmann, Liv/Gardli, Kristin/ Hasvold, Tove (2010): Empowerment: Ansikt til ansikt gir innsikt. Et forsøk på reelt samarbeid med brukere i de sosialfaglige utdanningene. Empowerment i sosialfagutdanningene – mye prat lite ull? [Empowerment: 'Meeting Face to Face Creates Insights'. An attempt at substantial cooperation with users in the social work educational programmes. Empowerment in social work educational programmes]. *Fontene forskning*, 02, pp. 17-26.

Askheim, Ole Petter/Altmann, Liv/Hasvold, Tove (2014): «Ansikt til ansikt gir innsikt» – brukere som medstudenter i sosialfaglig utdanning ['"Meeting Face to Face Creates Insights']. I Gerd Bjørke, Harald Jarning/Olav Eikeland (Red.). *Ny praksis – ny kunnskap: om utviklingsarbeid som sjanger* [New practice – new knowledge: on developmental work as a genre] (pp. 190-201). Oslo: AMB-media.

Blaikie, Norman (1993): *Approaches to social inquiry*. Cambridge: Polity Press.

Coleridge, Peter. (1993): *Disability, Liberation and Development*. Oxford: Oxfam.

Freire, Paulo (1970): *Pedagogy of the oppressed*. New York: Herder/Herder.

Honneth, Axel (1996): *The Struggle for Recognition: The Moral Grammar of Social Conflicts*. Cambridge, Massachusetts: MIT Press Ltd.

Levine, Stephen K./Levine, Ellen G. (1999): *Foundations of Expressive Arts Therapy*. London: Jessica Kingsley.

Modig, Maria (1984): *Den nödvändiga olydnaden*. [*The Required Disobedience*]. Stockholm: Natur och kultur.

Robinson, Karen/Webber, Martin (2012): The Meaningful Involvement of Service Users and Carers in Advanced-Level Post-Qualifying Social Work Education: A Qualitative Study. *British Journal of Social Work* Volume 42, pp. 1256-1274.

Robinson, Karen/Webber, Martin (2013): Models and Effectiveness of Service User and Carer Involvement in Social Work Education: A literature Review. *British Journal of Social Work* Volume 43, pp. 925-944.

Starrin, Bengt (2007): Empowerment som livsinnstilling – kan vi lære noe av Pippi Langstrømpe? [Empowerment as an approach to life – can we learn something from Pippi Longstocking?] I Ole Petter Askheim/Bengt Starrin, (Red.): *Empowerment i teori og praksis* [*Empowerment as theory and practice*] (pp. 59- 71). Oslo: Gyldendal Akademisk.

3.3 England: Gap-Mending: Developing a New Approach to User and Carer Involvement in Social Work Education

Peter Beresford, Helen Casey and John MacDonough

The UK Context

Social work in the UK has a long history stretching back to the nineteenth century. Two overlapping and often conflicting strands in its development were utilitarian philanthropy, associated with pioneers like Octavia Hill and the settlement movement, linked with Canon Samuel and Henrietta Barnett. While the first was associated with the regulation of charity, the other sought to bridge the divide between privileged and disadvantaged people. The context for modern social work was the post-war welfare state with its commitment to social citizenship and the equalization of opportunity (Beresford 2016).

Social work underwent an expansion in the 1970s. Again we can see conflicting strands in its development. In the early 1970s there were pressures to bureaucratization, professionalization and managerialism associated with the creation of local authority social services departments. By the mid 1970s the 'radical social work' movement had emerged to challenge this, committed to participation and structural change through social work. This gave further impetus to a social work committed to challenging inequality and discrimination, supporting social justice and valuing diversity. This was reflected both in the formal structures of social work as well as the increasing right-wing political and media opposition social work encountered (Bailey/Brake 1975).

However, the two conflicting ideologies, that embodied in identity-based movements, including the disabled people's and service user movement, and that committed to the private market, embodied in increasingly powerful neoliberalism, had one important meeting point in public policy. This was a new common interest in public participation and user involvement. Social work was at the vanguard of this development and by the early 1990s had established provisions for user involvement in policy and practice (Beresford/ Croft 1990). A particularly important development was the pressure for more user (and carer[7]) involvement in social work *education* and when in 2003 social work education became degree based, such involvement became a requirement, supported with central funding, for all qualifying (and subsequently post-qualifying education and training) (Branfield 2009).

Presentation of the concept of the course

Such an approach to learning has become a gateway to participatory social work for both practitioners and service users. For those committed to emancipation, social work is, or should be concerned with working alongside people disempowered and oppressed in society, steeped in principles of human rights and social justice and the values of anti-discriminatory and anti-oppressive practice. This is what attracts many students into the profession; to work with people to "address the problems and difficulties in their lives" (SWAN 2009). Unfortunately, and for too many years now, this aspect of social work has been increasingly undermined by the managerialism, privatisation, 'austerity' and an ever growing dominance of market forces already touched on. Social workers themselves and social work students have also felt oppressed, through the encroachment of the 'marketisation' of their practice (Ferguson 2008). This has led to an increasing stigmatisation and pathologising of service users and carers, and an ever-widening gap between them and social work practitioners; anathema to those who value relationship based practice and effective partnership working.

There is, however, an antidote to this, and it lies in the effective involvement and active participation of service users and carers in the ongoing education of social work students and practitioners, which has been growing in scale and sophistication through the twenty first century. The reasons for this are manifold, as are the added value benefits of this involvement. Meaningful service user and carer involvement acts as consistent reminder to students and practitioners of the motivating factors that brought them into social work and the fact that emotional intelligence can be just as important as aca-

---

7   Carers are family member or friend providing unpaid support to someone close to them.

demic or analytical intelligence. It ensures that we never lose sight of the fact that that service users and carers are human beings (Advocacy in Action 2006; Branfield 2007; Morrow et al. 2012). As far back as 2006, Advocacy in Action identified that effective involvement also "provides valuable correctives to bureaucratic and procedure driven practice that can characterise much of statutory social work." (Advocacy in Action 2006: 342).

To bring these common goals to fruition has to involve a breaking down of the perceived, but often all too real, barriers between practitioners, students, academics, service providers and service users, and a mending of the gaps between them to produce social work courses fit for purpose.

"In social work education, more than in any other area, there are common aims between the individuals providing services, the teaching staff, the service users and the students. We should use these common aims to develop the courses together." (service user cited in Branfield 2007: 1)

Extensive research has been undertaken into how service users and carers are involved in social work education; some of the best of it emanating from the Social Care Institute for Excellence[8] and the service user umbrella organisation Shaping Our Lives. Much of this research has looked at the service user and carer experience and how it can be improved as well as the barriers and challenges that face academics and service users and carers when facilitating this vital aspect of a social worker's education. For example, Taylor, Braye and Cheng (2009) and Branfield (2009) highlight the fact that the sharing of information and improvement of supportive infrastructures are vital to sustainable involvement. Discussions are undertaken in their research, as well as in those of Beresford (2013) and Branfield, Beresford and Levin (2007), into the resourcing of service user and carer involvement; both in terms of payment for involvement, but also in terms of staff support. Interestingly these publications all stress the importance of reciprocity in terms of service user satisfaction; something that lies at the heart of the more recent gap-mending approach to teaching.

Gap-mending approaches began to underpin teaching at London South Bank University (LSBU) since 2012 and New College Durham (NCD) since

---

8 The Social Care Institute for Excellence is a charitable company independent of government in its operations although it receives core funding from government grants. The main aim of SCIE is to collate and disseminate knowledge about good practice in social care in the UK (SCIE 2002).

2014. In a professional learning context, service users, carers and students can learn together as partners.

Realisation, implementation, experiences

The introduction to 'gap-mending' approaches and involvement with PowerUs, has enabled us to realise the potential for changing the way service users are involved in the delivery of social work education and the range of different ways in which this can be realised. By creating a learning environment where people share their experiences and knowledge, traditional barriers that exist between people on the receiving end of professional support and those providing it can be removed.

The opportunity to implement this new approach to social work education at LSBU; came through the delivery of the module, 'Advocacy, Partnership and Participation' to second year undergraduate students. The module appeared to lend itself logically to this approach, as both partnership (Thompson 2003) and participation (Thompson 2003; Beresford 2012) are inextricably linked to the redressing of power differentials, enabling involvement in decision making; with participation being the active ingredient in effective partnership working (Thompson 2003). It is an active ingredient that inherently enables service users and carers to challenge "people's disempowerment and redistributing power and control." (Beresford 2012: 26). These concepts are also, according to Braye (2000: 9), integral and "defining features of the social care landscape".

The module content was consequently designed with this gap-mending pedagogical approach in mind, and was supported by the University, Health Care Professions Council (HCPC – regulatory body), and The College of Social Work (since closed due to removal of government funding). There is currently no formal accreditation of this module but it is an aim for future courses. Whilst approval is positive, as Bines and Watson (2006: 137) state "our own academic and personal values shape the pedagogical decisions we make", thus it was necessary to consider how best to prepare those involved for the challenges of this integrated gap-mending model of learning in social work education.

Taking this new approach felt innovative and creative; Burgess/Lawrence (2007) and Eadie/Lymbery (2007) who both highlight the virtues of creativity in social work education, explain that it has a direct correlation

with the creativity of the student, and ultimately of the social work practitioner, saying:
"I think it could be argued that creativity is a vital component of a good social worker. If creativity is looking outside the box, seeing things from a different perspective or experiencing oneself differently, then effectively doing and promoting these things in others are essential for good practice." (Burgess/Laurance 2007: 2)

To achieve this goal it was helpful to ascertain the perspectives of the prospective participants, with the use of focus groups the most appropriate option to obtain a range of views from people with potentially widely differing backgrounds (Bloor et al. 2001; Morgan/Krueger 1993).

There were three distinct groups participating; social work students, social work academics and service users and carers, with the latter being grouped together for convenience at this stage.

While the use of three focus groups is a convenient way of accessing data, it raises a question of how meaningful it can be in terms of being representative of any of the constituent groups. Whilst focus groups allow the group dynamics to bring out data that may otherwise have been unobtainable, there is always the risk that participants may hide their views (Whittaker 2012), or some members dominate discussions (Sarantakos 2013).

Additionally, the focus groups were small and the participants all known to the facilitator, which can potentially influence the reliability of the data (Bloor et al. 2001).

The findings of this initial research can be divided into four sections; corresponding to the four key questions asked in the focus groups.

- What do you see as being the positive aspects of student social workers learning alongside service users and carers in an integrated manner?
- What are the less positive aspects?
- What do you see as being the challenges to the success of this module?
- How can those challenges be addressed?

The discussions in all three groups appeared to be open and frank; perhaps as a result of the members of each group knowing each other. Participants all thought this the course was an innovative idea and were interested in its inception and background. One of the messages from all participants was that they understood that this way of teaching could act as a way of 'humanising' social work and social services.

> "I'm really looking forward to meeting interesting new people, maybe making new friends which I guess could open up ethical issues; but, what the hell, why not. Meeting people and getting to know about them is one of the reasons I'm studying this course, so the more the merrier." (Social Work Student1)

> "To be able to put away our given identities for a while and just all be students together." (Social Work Student 2)

All of the participants could see the educational value of this method of teaching:

> "I have helped to teach at universities; but I never thought I would have the chance to study at a university. This was something that would never happen to me, and now it might. I want to learn more so that I can become better at being myself and happier. This is good!" (Service User/Carer 1)

In terms of the less positive aspects there was an interesting correlation between the views of the service users and the student focus group. The main concerns voiced by the service users and student groups were centred around fear, in one form or another. As one of the social work students said, "I am a little worried that the service users might make judgements about me if I say something that they think is wrong." (Social Work student 2). While one of the service users, participant said:

> "I guess that the students will get to see me for who I am, and not just what I look like or what has happened to me in my life; though I am scared that they may know so much more than I do that I will not feel a part of the group, and I don't want to feel that way again." (Service User/Carer 1)

There was also a collective fear of failure and of letting themselves down as well as each other. The final fear expressed was one of commitment and workloads, and how they would manage this; for differing reasons in each group, but the fear was just the same.

> "How are the teaching staff going to be able to manage this number of students and provide the right levels of support the different people need to work safely and happily together?" (Social work student 1)

As to how the challenges could be addressed; this seemed to be the most difficult question, with each group struggling a little to work out what they could offer; but some very helpful advice was ultimately forthcoming. All three groups felt that effective communication and information sharing were crucial to the successful running of the module, and that any and all different ways of communicating must be embraced to ensure fairness.

"I don't have a computer at home or access to the internet, so if anyone needs to get hold of me outside university they would have to use my mobile. I'm very good with my mobile; in fact, I use it far too much." (Service User/Carer 4)

The groups also all felt that consistency from the teaching staff was very important. All participants were generous in their understanding that nothing is perfect, and that as long as communication is clear and transparent, mistakes can be tolerated. The service user group, student and staff groups all felt that the first session was probably going to be crucial to establishing how successful or not the module would be; including in this the information shared in the build-up. In fact two of the staff members and a service user came up with an idea, mirroring the model pioneered at Lund University, Sweden, to have an away-day, where all the students could get together and get to know each other, prior to sitting down and studying; breaking down barriers in a neutral setting.

The module lasted for 12 weeks, with sessions of three hours duration taking place once a week and consisting of a taught element in a lecture theatre; followed by group work, where mixed groups of up to six social work students and service users/carers worked together to create a virtual social enterprise, reflecting the principles of advocacy, partnership working and participation. In total, fifty four service user students and eighty two social work students have participated in these modules. The aim of the group work was also to live out the principles of advocacy, partnership, and empowerment; with participants encouraging participation from each other. As Adams (2008) makes clear, however, participation itself is no absolute guarantee of empowerment – but it usually helps and service users or carers need "to be empowered in order to participate, or at least be likely to become empowered through participating" (Adams 2008: 29). It was also hoped the participants would learn from each other's knowledge and experience, and break down any barriers or pre-conceived views they might have. The module culminated in group presentations to a panel of experts and poster presentations reflecting individual's journeys through the module.

In contrast to the approach taken at London South Bank University, at New College Durham the first gap-mending programme was piloted in response to barriers identified by service users. Social work students on placement at a children's centre were prevented from joining parents who felt very negative about social workers. As one parent later explained:

"When you hear the words 'social worker', it fills you with so much fear that you want to run a mile." (Service user participant 1)

In discussion with the children's centre manager a voluntary meeting was offered to explore the barrier that clearly existed between parents and social workers. Nine out of a potential 12 parents came to the first meeting which established the beginning of 'mending the gap' between parents and professionals'.

The group of parents who attended four meetings, to plan and develop a gap-mending programme, consisted of seven mothers and two fathers. All had different experiences and different stories to tell, but they were united by the common experience of having lost, or been separated from their children by social workers.

It was fantastic to see how motivated these parents were to have their voice heard on a subject that provoked deep and difficult emotions. They demonstrated through dialogue how much experience can inform learning.

Common ground identified in the first meeting included agreement by parents that: The best experience of social work intervention led to children being placed in a safe environment.

They went on to share their worst experiences:

- poor/ negative communication – one parent described herself and her child being reduced to tears by the way they were spoken to
- not being prepared – different social workers going over the same information, making each visit time consuming
- bringing up the past – even where the outcome was positive, there were many strong views shared about the use of past history against people, as one father observed:

"Why send us on courses to change our behaviour if they are going to keep going on about our past...makes you think, why bother? They are never going to see us any differently." (Service user participant 2)

Parents agreed that a better approach would include:

- professionals saying things differently, as one mother recalled:

"I'll never forget the way the social worker spoke to me, as if I wasn't even a human being, let alone a mother to my children. She made me feel this (fingers demonstrating extremely small) big."

- believing people can change (echoing earlier comment above)
- advocacy support, as explained by a mother new to the area:

  "I knew nobody and just wanted some support from someone who understood what I was going through, who could support me with getting my points across. I have managed to do this, but it is not easy when you are upset and stressed"

- information explained better – everyone agreed that they were not sufficiently informed about relevant matters, processes, or their rights, often due to complicated terminology/letters or professionals "just not bothering to tell you anything"
- there was some agreement that the information focus was on the child, therefore it didn't really matter if parents did not understand, again reinforcing their feeling of being invisible.

Parents felt that generally they feared speaking up for themselves at meetings and had felt "invisible":

It was agreed that some important gaps had been identified which needed to be mended. Over three further meetings the content of the programme was planned, which was key to empowering parents as pioneers in this exciting project. For the first time in their experience they were not joining something where others had pre-determined the content. In this context, social work students would be recruited as co-participants. Eight social work students and one community health student from new College Durham took part, resulting in a balance in numbers between parents and students. Emphasis was placed on their commitment to the programme. A central philosophy to the gap-mending approach is for people to meet as *people first*. Therefore the course began with an introductory activity to enable participants to come together prior to teaching sessions. Parents chose to meet with students for the first time at the children's centre, as it was an environment that they were familiar with and felt comfortable in. For the same reason all the sessions were held there. Each session was three hours: 10am-1pm. As a pilot programme it was not validated, therefore attendance was optional and without accreditation. However, the reward for commitment, participation and success was made with a certificate of attendance and celebration event.

Discussion at the first session developed naturally over tea, coffee and cake which became a theme of the gap-mending sessions.

The programme content was introduced to students by parents and the main themes of the gap-mending sessions agreed:

- week one – introduction/activity
- week two – establishing ground rules/confidentiality/communication
- week three – professional standards, Role of the Health and Care Professions and The College of Social work
- week four – presentation skills and reflection
- week five – advocacy and empowerment
- week six – professional values, medical/social model
- week seven – emotional well being/resilience, relaxation
- week eight – presentations, evaluation/defining project outcomes and new opportunities
- week nine – celebration of achievement/certificate event.

The themes of these sessions were largely informed by the gaps identified by parents at the first meeting. However, what brought them to life were the discussions which involved sharing both experiences and learning together. Examples include:

a) Written communication
In one exercise students were asked to write a letter to parents to arrange an initial meeting. A brief outline was provided about the parent they were writing to and the letters were signed with different names so that the students could not be identified. Parents read the letters and provided feedback based upon several factors:

- how they would feel receiving the letter
- examples of good and bad practice within the letter
- how the letter could be improved upon.

Interestingly, what most students realised was how detached they were from written communication; they had observed that generally within social work departments the administrative staff sent a letter without social workers signing or even reading them. They agreed that this was something they needed to follow up and discuss at their placements. They agreed to feedback at the following session about suggestions they had made for improving written communication, such as:

- writing the letters themselves
- ensuring that the correct term of reference is used in the introduction (i.e. not using first name)
- explaining who they are, their role and the purpose of a meeting
- providing options of where to meet, date and time
- providing contact details and signing the letter.

b) Supervised contact

This is where a parent has time-limited contact with their child/children arranged by a social worker. It often involves someone the child or parent has never met before taking the child to the social services venue where they would spend time with another parent. The meeting would be observed and recorded by the social worker who does not explain the purpose of taking notes or what they are writing about. Both parents and social work students explained their lack of understanding of why this is the standard process and how uncomfortable this experience is for all concerned. At this stage in the gap-mending programme, we were attracting interest from the local children and families' team and invited a social worker to come and join the discussion about how this could change and be a much better experience for all involved.

Evaluations, critical reflections

On completion of the course at LSBU the same focus groups were gathered together and the findings divided again into four sections; corresponding to the four key questions asked in the focus groups (identified earlier).

The feedback from all groups was enthusiastic and that the course was an overwhelmingly positive experience; with all participants valuing the opportunity of learning together and from each other, sharing different perspectives, and breaking down barriers, building bridges and encouraging a sense of equality. For example:

> "That's what I liked and that's what I think was so positive about this course; that I am an equal to the social workers. In the past they have not treated me as an equal and have made me feel really insignificant and not good, and this was a concern of mine beforehand." (Service User / Carer Participant 2)

Service users, carers and social work students felt that learning and working together was the best way they had experienced of overcoming pre-conceived ideas and demystifying people's fear of the unknown. Both sets of participants firmly believed that this fully integrated way of working of working was the only way they had experienced of truly eliminating the sense of a 'them and us'. They felt that eradicating this attitude was crucial to being able to uphold the values of social work and avoid the possibility of "causing the all too familiar faces of stigma and discrimination from the very people who should know better." (Moreland 2007, cited in Ferguson/Woodward 2009: 127).

All participants greatly valued the opportunity they were given to work in a very different way, and felt that humanising each other would help them in the future. Service users and carers would be less sceptical and see social workers as human beings and social work students more likely to understand just how much knowledge, understanding and insight service users and carers brought to partnership working. This has been recognised in research undertaken by Taylor, Braye and Cheng (2009), who found that social work education would clearly be enhanced by "creating spaces" (Taylor/Braye/Cheng 2009: 53) that enabled social work students and service users and carers to be able to explore their similarities and differences; "to enable students to engage with the complexity of the personal and professional relationships involved" (Taylor/Braye/Cheng 2009: 53).

One of the most striking conclusions from the service users and carers was the fact that they now understood that these students wanted to make a difference and to help them to help themselves and improve their lives, and that this was why they came into social work.

> "I feel bad now that I had such negative views of social workers, and never really saw the human being behind the job; when it is actually the job that seems to be the problem. I found out social workers can have very similar life experiences to me, which was eye opening." (Service User/Carer 4)

Service users and carers also reported that the course had given them the confidence to speak for themselves and challenge power differentials and the skills to work alongside professionals to achieve better outcomes for themselves and their families. They felt empowered; that they had had become powerful. Adams' (2008) explanation of this process certainly appeared to apply to this group of people through the process of undertaking this module.

They had taken ownership of their situations, used their knowledge and power to challenge disadvantage, inequality and oppression and made positive differences to the quality of their own lives and those of their families.

"I was able to use the language of the professionals and apply the knowledge of advocacy I had gained to speak up for my son and present his needs in such a way that he now has the specific residential care that is required to meet his needs. I do not think this would have happened if I had not gained the confidence to talk to these people as my equal." (Service user/carer 4)

Mirroring this were the comments from the social work students who all said that the experience had helped them in their work with service users and carers on placement and in other job roles.

"My instant thought now is to get the views of the service users I am working with and encourage them to actively participate in anything we are doing, from assessments to working out timetables. My practice and the outcomes of that practice are already better." (Social work student 5)

In terms of the less positive aspects and challenges the participants faced, they were all around structural and organisational issues, and nothing to do with the underpinning principles and nature of the course. These comments came from all participants and the unified nature of their response reflected other similarities between the students and service users and carers. Students' experiences of vulnerability and powerlessness within the university could be compared with service user experiences of social services, and how similar these experiences are. An extrapolation of this is the fact that in this marketised age service users are very often referred to as customers; whilst as Morley (2003: 129) points out, "in a market economy, students are no longer constructed as recipients of welfare, but purchasers of an expensive product."

This was brought home by both these focus groups voicing the fact that they expected a quality of service provision and support when they needed it, and that just being offered something as a passive recipient was not good enough anymore.

Applying the gap-mending approach to this module not only changed the way the service users, carers and social work students viewed each other and their roles within society; it changed the way as a teacher work can be viewed. By really seeing the difference such integrated partnership working could make to work in education but in social work practice as well; as it really is all about the relationships that we build, no matter what role we are undertaking, that make a difference to our practice.

> "It is in the plans and dreams of these fragile but visionary movements that we get a glimpse of just how different relationships between professional social workers and people who use services could be." (Ferguson 2008: 87)

This was demonstrated at the end of the gap-mending programme between parents and professional students from NCD. The evaluation process was based upon the key messages parents and students learned from each other.

Some key messages from parents to students:

- Think out of the box, rather than tick boxes/categories – have an open mind.
- Don't be a text book social worker – use theory/legislation/guidelines, but use your own initiative/judgement.
- Don't be judgemental/ be personable and professional.
- Do question/challenge, even if you think your manager will say 'no', at least you have tried.
- Don't have a "stinking" attitude, e.g. a social worker should not tell parents what to do, they should give them choices based on things they can do.
- If a parent tells you they are struggling e.g. with addiction, give help/support – admitting should be a positive thing, not negative.
- Don't just focus on the child; focus on parents and families as a whole
- Give parents achievable goals.
- If a parent gets angry, upset – think about why, there will be a good reason.

Some key messages from students to parents:

- Don't be afraid to co-operate with services and be willing to develop productive relationships.
- Always ask if you do not understand anything within the process to ensure you understand what is involved as part of your assessments.
- We are on a learning journey and value your shared experiences and acknowledge the importance of these in your lives; we have appreciated the time parents have taken to be involved in our learning.

- Parents have allowed us to explore our feelings about their experiences in a non-judgemental and safe environment and we want to let you know that this way of learning and exploration of feelings and values continues outside of our sessions.

Other outcomes include:

- initiating a creative writing group who are working towards publishing a gap-mending poetry book
- participation in the first PowerUs film shown at a European social work conference
- establishing 'Parentkind', a parent-led service working with social services to facilitate consultation and feedback with other parents and provide peer advocacy support, also exploring links with nurse training and education.

One key outcome for a small group of parents and students has been their increased confidence, which has enabled them to respond to the wide interest about this project. They have been interviewed by BBC radio and have had an article published about them in a national newspaper. The outcomes from this first pilot programme have inspired further programmes:

- The Higher Education Academy funded an event to explore how gaps could be mended with young people, which has led to the development of the second gap-mending programme at New College Durham.
- Sunderland University social work department ran their first gap-mending programme in partnership with Sunderland carers centre.
- New College Durham will soon be launching the next gap-mending programme in partnership with Investing in People and Culture and the Scottish Refugee Council in order to mend the gaps between asylum seekers, refugees and a wider range of students in health and care professional education.

Further exploration of the impact and transferability of this approach within other contexts will be made within future programmes.

A further aim for NCD and LSBU is to investigate accreditation for the programmes to enable participants to acquire credits.

At LSBU, the gap-mending principles have been applied in the area of student practice education. LSBU in partnership with 'My Support Workers

Ltd.' (MSW) are working on the co-production of placements offering unique opportunities for students to work alongside service users, carers and allied health professions to apply the gap-mending principles to learning with and from each other, developing innovative service solutions.

We are utilising the practical partnership approaches of co-production (Hunter/Ritchie 2007), underpinned by the principles of gap-mending to enable service users, carers, students and practice educators to work together to co-produce inspiring social work placements that challenge, educate and empower all involved as equal partners. This project mends the gaps through placements that provide:

- co-learning spaces between service users. Students and practitioners
- opportunities for all participants to make sense of their experiential learning as a resource for effective personal systems and change
- enhanced learning opportunities and the practical application of students and practitioners through direct access to lived experience
- opportunities for co-creating new knowledge and emerging learning paradigms.

It was found that teaching social work students, service users and carers together in mutual learning situations results in more equal and improved practice. The benefits of seeing all participants as partners in learning and the benefits of participatory research enhances the potential for improving practice.

Conclusion

There are strongly competing strands in modern UK social work, as there have been in social work from its early founding. There are currently strong ideological and political pressures to privatisation, managerialism and increased managerial control, as well as an emphasis on academic ability and the need for 'elite' social work education courses to feed this perceived need for more closely controlled practice and provision. At the same time, neoliberal politics have emphasised the importance of reducing state spending, cutting public services and getting people off welfare benefits into employment. This has been associated with the increased stigmatisation and 'othering' of groups like lone and poor parents, disabled people and mental health service users, refugees and asylum seekers; groups that are also closely associated with receipt of social work services. The effect of these developments is to privilege the control rather than support role of social work and emphasise the distance between service users, practitioners and citizens more generally. We can see from the pioneering initiatives that have developed in the UK the part that a gap-mending approach in social work (and indeed potentially in other helping professions) may play in challenging the divisions that are increasingly being highlighted politically, and rehumanising social work as well as other health and care professions.

In the UK, for example, divisions between people who are reliant on welfare benefits and people in paid employment, characterised by some politicians and media as skivers and strivers respectively, have been played up by right wing politicians and media. The same has been done to distance citizens from refugees and asylum seekers and so on. Social work practice and practitioners correspondingly are being increasingly distanced from the people they work with by the imposition of layers of bureaucracy, rationing processes that include mechanical call centres and prewritten scripts in the 'assessment' process and practitioners who have to spend more and more time in front of computer screens, recording the minutiae of their activities.

The gap-mending approach highlights that there is an alternative and the evidence we already have – although it needs to be built on – indicates that it is valued by both service users and providers and can achieve the formal personal and social goals established for social work. Based on the idea of supporting understanding, contact and relationship between service users and workers, it provides a critical starting point for relationship based social work in preliminary learning that models such a relationship in its own process. It offers a much bigger international beacon for progressive and effective social work learning and practice that offers an effective challenge to the regressive direction of travel of social work under neo-liberal politics and ideology.

References

Adams, R. (2008): Empowerment, participation and social work: fourth edition, Basingstoke: Palgrave MacMillan.
Advocacy in Action (June 2006): 'Making it Our Own Ball Game: Learning and Assessment in Social Work Education',In: Social Work Education 25 (4), pp. 332-346.

Banks, S. (2006): Ethics and values in social work: third edition, Basingstoke: Palgrave MacMillan.
Beresford, P. and Croft, S. (1990): From Paternalism To Participation: Involving people in social services, (1990), London, Joseph Rowntree Foundation and Open Services Project.
Beresford, P. (2016): All Our Welfare: Towards participatory social policy, Bristol, Policy Press.
Beresford, P. (2012): The theory and philosophy behind user involvement, in Beresford, P./Carr, S. (eds) Social care, service users and user involvement, London: Jessica Kingsley, pp. 21-36.
Beresford, P. (2013): Beyond the usual suspects: towards inclusive user involvement, London: Shaping Our Lives.
Beresford, P./Boxall, K. (2012): 'Service Users, Social Work education and knowledge for Social Work Practice': In Social Work Education, Vol 31, No 2, pp. 155-167.
Beresford, P./Croft, S. (2008): 'Democratising Social Work – a key element of innovation: from "client" as object, to service user as producer',in The Innovation Journal: The Public Sector Innovation Journal, Vol 13, No 1, pp. 5-22.
Biggs, J./Tang, C. (2011): Teaching for quality learning at university: fourth edition, Maidenhead: McGraw-Hill.
Bloor, M., et al (2001): Focus groups in social research, London: Sage.
Branfield, F. (February 2007): User involvement in social work education, London: Social Care Institute for Excellence.
Branfield, F. (2009): Developing User Involvement In Social Work Education, Workforce Development Report 29, London, Social Care Institute for Excellence.
Branfield, F., Beresford, P., and Levin, L. (2007): Common aims: a strategy to support service user involvement in social work education, London: Social Care Institute for Excellence.
Braye, S. (2000): Participation and involvement in social care. In Kemshall, H./ Littlechild, R. (eds) User involvement and participation in social care: research informing practice. London: Jessica Kingsley, pp. 9-28.
Brown, K., et al (2008) Developing the active and informed participation of people who use services in the design, delivery and assessment of learning and development provision for the social care workforce in the Skills for Care South West Region, Bournemouth: Bournemouth University.
Burgess, H./Laurance, J. (2007): Reflections on Creativity in Social Work and Social Work Education Disciplinary Perspectives on Creativity in higher Education, [online] 13 Oct 2008. Available from: http://www.heacademy.ac.uk/creativity. htm [accessed on 8th January 2016].
Eadie, T./Lymbery, M. (2007): Promoting Creative Practice Through Social Work Education, in Social Work Education, 26 (7), pp. 670-683.
Ferguson, I. (2008): Reclaiming social work: challenging neo-liberalism and promoting social justice, London: Sage.

Ferguson, I./Woodward, R. (2009): Radical social work in practice: making a difference, Bristol: The Policy Press.
Hart, E./Bond, M. (1999): Action research for health and social care: a guide to practice, Buckingham: Open University Press.
Hodge, S. (2005): 'Participation, Discourse and Power: a Case Study in Service User Involvement', *Critical Social Policy*, 25 (2), pp. 164-179.
Hunter, S./Ritchie, P. (2007): With, not to: models of co-production in social welfare in Hunter, S./Ritchie, P. (eds) Co-production and personalisation in social care: changing relationships in the provision of social care, London: Jessica Kingsley Publishers.
Morley, L. (2003): Quality and power in higher education, Maidenhead: Open University Press.
Morrow, E. et al (2012): Handbook of service user involvement in nursing and healthcare research, Chichester: Wiley-Blackwell.
PowerUs (2016): Networking PowerUs. [online] available at http://www.powerus.se/ [accessed 8th January 2016].
Sarantakos, S. (2013): Social Research: fourth edition, Basingstoke: Palgrave MacMillan.
SCIE (2002): Introducing the Social Care Institute for Excellence (SCIE). [online] available at http://docs.scie-socialcareonline.org.uk/fulltext/75648.pdf [accessed 18th January 2016].
SCIE (2011*) 'We are more than our story': service user and* carer participation in social work education, London: Social Care Institute for Excellence.
SWAN (2009) The Social Work Action Network constitution,[online] available at http://socialworkfuture.org/who-we-are/constitution [accessed 8th January 2016].
Taylor, I., Braye, S./Cheng, A. (2009) Carers as partners *(CaPs)* in social work education, London: Social Care Institute for Excellence.
Thompson, N. (2003) Promoting equality: challenging discrimination and oppression, second edition, Basingstoke: Palgrave MacMillan.
Walker, M. (2006) Higher Education Pedagogies, Maidenhead: Open University Press
Whittaker, A. (2012) Research skills for social work: second edition, Exeter: Sage.

3.4 Denmark: Interdisciplinary Gap-Mending Courses as Part of R&D Projects at the Metropolitan University College

Ann Rasmussen and Camusa Hatt

Context of two interdisciplinary gap-mending courses

In Denmark, the Metropolitan University College has completed three variations of user involving courses inspired by gap-mending methods. This chapter discusses the two latest gap-mending courses, which were conceived as an integrated part of a large public-private innovation project in which Metropolitan was a partner: OPALL[9]. Being embedded in a larger research and development (R&D) project entailed a unique opportunity for developing and testing different concepts for user involving innovation courses.

The immediate occasion for these user involvement courses, was thus to contribute to the overall OPALL project purpose: Developing solutions to selected municipal welfare challenge, through cross-sector collaboration.

In the first of these courses, the users were Danish veterans with mental injuries caused by participation in international crisis and war actions on behalf of Denmark. The users in this course participated on exact equal terms with the Metropolitan students. In the second case, the users were refugees and immigrants from non-western countries, living in social housing estates. Also these users participated in the gap-mending course on equal grounds with the Metropolitan students. However, as will be discussed in later sections, the form of user involvement was adjusted.[10]

The students participating in the courses were in the last part of their Bachelor's Degree programmes in Social Work, Nursing, Occupational Therapy and other welfare study programmes.

---

9 OPALL is the Danish abbreviation for Public-Private Alliances
10 In this chapter, we use the term "users" and "user involvement" rather than "service users" and "service user involvement". This is the most widely used in Denmark; and conveys a focus on the wider user context, rather than merely on his/her role as user of a particular service.

In each course, an interdisciplinary team of teachers[11] was established, where each teacher had specific competences regarding innovation, pedagogic and/or the chosen challenge.

The course was planned as a 6 week innovation course, where students from different disciplines develop ideas for improving a product or service. This concept was an established part of the Metropolitan curriculum.

Given that the overall objective of the innovation course was to provide new solutions to a specific welfare challenge, it was natural to involve the users. Specifically within the fields of social innovation and innovating public services, i.e. the context of the courses, user driven or user involving innovation is widely acknowledged and used.

The users are seen as an important driver of innovating public services, by giving insight into the real user needs and challenges. The users are furthermore seen as important co-creators of new ideas and solutions to the challenges, through their participation in idea-development and design of prototypes (co-creating) (Bason 2010). Finally the users are involved in testing and evaluating the ideas and the prototypes.

In the R&D context of the two user involvement courses described in this chapter, the purpose of involving the users in the courses is to ensure more comprehensive and suitable services, and thus increased value for the user of the public service. From an innovation perspective, empowerment of the involved users is thus seen as a desirable and wished-for side-effect of the user involvement.

Users have thus been involved on a regular basis in Metropolitan's innovation courses. Typically as informants, interviewed and observed by students to explore the users' needs, challenges and ideas for new solutions. Later the students would typically present the users with the refined ideas and prototypes to get the users' feedback.

However, the courses presented in this chapter implied a much more radical form of user involvement, where the users participated on more equal ground with the students.

The inspiration came from the Metropolitan Social Work degree programme, where the first gap-mending course had just been completed in May 2013, inspired by colleagues at Lund University and the PowerUs network.

---

11 In this chapter we choose the term "teacher", covering different functions of e.g. project leader, counsellor and lecturer.

Based on the success of this course, the objective of the user involving courses was now expanded from "merely" increasing the quality of the course participants' proposals – to now also creating improved courses of study for the students, and empowering the user participants.

The courses presented in this chapter were planned with the pedagogical intention that not only a specific academic content was to be taught, supporting the students in achieving relevant knowledge, skills and competencies. The ambition was furthermore that the students should be challenged, engaged and motivated. It has been essential to the courses that the learning processes should be facilitated through a very close link between theory and practice – "practice" in this case being users, service providers, and volunteers.

Welfare challenges often require interdisciplinary solutions, involving cooperation between professionals from several disciplines and cooperation between different sectors. Therefore, in Denmark we see an explicit political demand for the educational institutions to deliver courses where students from different professions can learn with, from and about each other (Danish Education and Research Committee 2014). Such courses can be characterised as Interprofessional Education (IPE), as formulated by the Centre for the Advancement of Interprofessional Education (CAIPE):

> "Interprofessional Education occurs when two or more professions learn with, from and about each other to improve collaboration and the quality of care" (CAIPE 2002).

Thus, welfare study programmes must facilitate students' development of competencies that can meet the future challenges of increased interprofessional and cross-sectional collaborative practice. The need for these competencies are expressed in Danish political proposals and reforms in the field of e.g. social work and pedagogy cf. the Children's Reform 2011 and Primary School Reform, 2014.

As such, there is wide political recognition that interprofessional competencies are a central learning outcome for students of the welfare study programmes. And in interprofessional collaborative practice, user involvement is a key feature. Interprofessional Collaborative Practice (IPC) can thus be defined as:

> "Working in partnership between professions and/or between organisations with individuals, families, groups and communities" (CAIPE 2013: 3).

Thereby IPC points toward empowerment processes, in that it is both considered crucial that the "user's voice" is heard, and in the way that the perspective of the user is actively integrated in the process (Lauvås 2011). When the focus is upon IPC, robust professional competencies alone are not enough. Practicing IPC, the professionals must be able to recognise their professional role and their strengths and constraints. They must be able to reflect upon, or even set aside their specific professional perspectives and interests in order to develop shared knowledge and achieve synergy with the common goal of reaching the best possible solution for the users. These are also some of the challenges of ICP.

The courses presented have been placed in the later parts of the students' educational course, whereby the students at the outset of the courses already had solid professional competencies; had achieved a high level of certainty of themselves as professionals; and had the maturity to cooperate actively with users. The courses therefore represented a relevant field for the students in which they could activate their specific professional competencies and at the same time engage in IPC.

Thus the expectations to the two user involving courses were considerable. The two courses reflect different concepts of gap-mending methods, with insights from the first course integrated in the second course. We have therefore decided to treat them separately, so the first two sections discuss the concept and the implementation experiences of the first user involvement course, while the last two sections discuss concept and reflections from the second course. Finally we discuss evaluations and critical reflections across the two gap-mending courses.

Concept and realisation of courses

As mentioned above, the two user involving courses conducted in autumn 2013 and spring 2015, respectively, were focussed on developing services for veterans with mental injuries, and on improved health initiatives for social housing tenants with refugee and immigrant backgrounds.

The two courses had many similarities: 1) the objective to contribute to one specific municipal welfare challenge, 2) the users in the courses thus representing the chosen welfare challenge, 3) the courses being interdisciplinary representing 3-6 different welfare study programs, 4) the team of teachers for each course representing different disciplines, and 5) the courses being formed as 5- or 6-weeks innovation courses. Finally both courses entailed expectations of an after-life for the developed proposals.

From a didactical perspective, the vision was to establish "second degree gap-mending": As a means of strengthening the students' skills as future social and healthcare workers, the students were offered theory, tools and hands-on experience in creating better welfare solutions to real-life challenges. This entailed also working together with 1) the users, with whom they as future professionals will be working for and together with, and 2) the students from other professions, with whom they will be collaborating in order to provide the best service to these users, i.e. engaging in interprofessional collaborative practice.

In spite of the many common concepts shared between the two courses, the *forms* of user involvement in the two gap-mending courses were in fact quite different, as the following sections will show.

Concept of the extracurricular course: The veteran innovation project

In the autumn of 2013, Metropolitan conducted the extracurricular gap-mending course "The veteran innovation project (VIP)". The goal of the course was to contribute with new services or improvement of existing services to the increasing number of Danish veterans with serious psychological injuries, including posttraumatic stress disorder, after participating in international war or peace keeping missions for the Danish state (e.g. in Ex-Yugoslavia, Afghanistan, Iraq).

The Danish municipalities had recently been imposed to implement a "veteran policy" to cater for war veterans. The media were providing frequent examples of neglect and lack of suitable services, paired with a rise in the number of veterans with mental injuries entailing large personal implications for the affected veterans and their families. For the municipalities this also has economic implications with young men shifting from working force members to dependents of welfare support.

The course was planned as a 6-week innovation course with an interdisciplinary team of students. Using gap-mending methods implied inviting users – i.e. veterans and next of kin – to participate in the full 6 week course on equal terms with the Metropolitan students. Due to the context of the course, being embedded as part of a larger R&D project, the course was planned as an extracurricular activity. Implementing new interdisciplinary types of curricular courses takes time, and was thus not deemed feasible.

The progression of the course followed a normal innovation process: from exploring the user needs and understanding the real challenge; to idea-development; prototyping workshop and implementation planning; with a presentation of the refined proposals at the Final.

During the 6 weeks, the students and veterans would participate in workshops, group work and receive presentations from Metropolitan teachers and guest speakers on topics such as post-traumatic stress, services offered by local and national government authorities, prototyping methods etc. As a general rule, attendance was required two days a week, covering workshops, presentations, group work and counselling by the 3 teachers. The rest was up to each group. The groups would be formed as interdisciplinary teams with both students and users, during the first day of the "future workshops", held as a 2-day stay in a rural setting.

Prior to the course kick-off, the planning group recruited the Metropolitan students, the veterans and next of kin, and finally a public service provider. During the course the participants were referred to as internal and external students. In this chapter we use the terms users and students.

Recruiting a service provider as an involved course "client" was seen as an advantage for several reasons: Firstly it could ensure easy access and insight into the service provider's objectives and institutional framework for delivering services to veterans' challenges. Secondly, it would potentially increase the chance of implementing proposals from the course. Thirdly, it could provide the course with direction, ensuring that the proposals helped meet an acknowledged municipal welfare challenge. Finally, having a service provider as client was expected to increase the motivation for both the participating students and users; knowing that a service provider was interested in the result of their course efforts.

Metropolitan thus invited a large municipality with a large number of war veterans to participate as clients of the veteran gap-mending course. The municipality (hereafter called the service provider) immediately accepted the invitation, as they were curious to gain insight into a new user group, with whom they had little experience – but had recently experienced political pressure to provide services to.

Metropolitan furthermore extended an invitation to participate as co-client to one of the veterans' trade unions, at the time very present in the public media with criticism of the lack of municipal services for the special needs of young veterans with psychological injuries. They were very encouraged by the gap-mending approach and also immediately agreed to the co-client role.

The goal was to recruit 12 Metropolitan students and an equal number of veterans. The students would be recruited through Metropolitan's intranet, combined with encouragement from teachers on selected relevant modules. Each student was asked to send a brief personal application. Recruitment of the veterans and next of kin was planned to be conducted through postings on billboards of veterans' meeting facilities. The teachers had a brief talk with each applicant, followed by an information meeting for the students and the users respectively.

Realization experiences of the veteran innovation course

The course started with 12 students from Metropolitan covering six different study degree programmes: physiotherapy, occupational therapy, nursing, social work, emergency and risk management, and nutrition and health.

Recruiting the users, the veterans and next of kin, proved to be more complicated than expected. Some key reflections are shared below. The teachers soon found that normal means of recruitment were not applicable in order to reach the veterans with psychological injuries, which is still considered a taboo by large sections of the soldiers and veterans. Instead it proved to be very efficient to e.g. tap into social media with a posting in one of the veteran groups on facebook, or contacting a veteran known from the media and tapping in to his wide network.

The teachers were then contacted by many users, who were grateful for the chance to be heard and make a difference. However, many were uncertain whether they could commit and actually show up for the full course. Eight users and one next of kin started the course; more had committed, but withdrew at the last minute before the course started.

Inviting so-called vulnerable user groups to attend gap-mending courses is time-consuming, involving many personal talks with users, both prior to and during the course. However, as elaborated below, this was indeed worth the time and efforts for all parties.

In the following we reflect on experiences with a few selected course elements: the future workshop, the prototype workshop and guest lectures by service providers.

The two-day future workshop in a rural vicinity allowed the participants to meet on more neutral ground, in an informal atmosphere, and over an intense period of time. For both users and students, the three phases (Criticism, Dreaming and Realisation) were challenging. In the criticism phase, the users were "in the lead" and the most active, since the overall theme of the course was improvement for mentally injured veterans. It demanded some courage to give insight into the challenges they experience with mental reactions, on a personal daily basis and in meetings with "the system". During the next more vision- and solution-focussed phases, the students found themselves back in the comfort zone. Also for the teachers, it was a very intense and demanding part of the course, making efforts to create an environment of trust.

The prototype workshop was a powerful method of creating, testing and giving feedback on tangible expressions of the participants' ideas for new or improved services. Here both users and students could convey their personal and professional experiences and insights in a more vivid form (acting out in role play, building paper models etc.).

The guest lectures by service providers proved to be a valuable meeting between the users and service providers. It thus reflected a shift in the "balance of power" and a form of empowerment of the users: The users could for the first time see themselves take on a more professional role as interviewers and hosts on neutral ground, with the service provider as the guest in the defensive role.

For each of the guest service providers (including the client), this was an unusually critical audience, where it soon became clear, that the users had much at stake personally. The service provider representatives in effect became target for years of frustration from several users, whereas the students had a more professional distance. The students have later conveyed, that this was a somewhat challenging experience for them to be part of – seeing the co-students personally affected. Also for the teachers it demanded efforts to facilitate an atmosphere of constructive dialogue.

For the users, the meeting with the service providers was somewhat disillusioning, having gained insight into how policies are implemented into services that do not necessarily cater to the users' needs.

At the same time the meetings provided new knowledge and transparency: A national government service provider, specifically responsible for meeting veterans' challenges, presented their attractive service offerings. However none of the users in the course had heard of this unit, in spite of years of desperate research to find this sort of support provided. The agency, who acknowledged not knowing how to market their services to the users, were provided with many innovative suggestions, including using the users as ambassadors:

> "We all know, who needs help, and who is on the verge of committing suicide; Why not let us help you market your organisation through our own channels" (i.e. closed facebook groups).

While despairing to some users, for others the meeting with the service providers also brought the insight that the personal frustrations after meeting "the system" were due to structural reasons, and thus not a personal failure. Unfortunately the disappointment from meeting the client was reinforced, when due to new urgent political priorities they were prevented from participating in the expert panel at the final presentation of proposals. However, the teachers were later invited to present the course experiences and proposals to the client's network of employees with responsibility for veterans. Timing did not allow for users to be part of the presentation, unfortunately. The client expressed acknowledgement and interest in the results and in the approach of contacting and mobilising resources even in users who were seriously impacted by PTSD.

The gap-mending course led to some fruitful experiences regarding motivation and commitment of both the users and the students. In evaluations the users have expressed that the course had been extremely demanding for them personally, but that they were grateful to have participated, including because of the self-insight they gained regarding their own hidden strengths.

For the users, veterans and the next of kin, the course was focused on their own real life challenges, which they had to deal with every day. This was not just an academic course, but a chance to reflect on and try to improve the situation for themselves and their fellow users. For the students this fact alone was a strong motivational factor, demanding extra commitment to the course in order to contribute to improved services for their temporary co-students, the users.

The strong personal commitments and consequent bonding between the users and students, also implies some *ethical issues*. For the students, the next course starts directly after the end of the gap-mending course, so they naturally have new priorities. For the users, there is a potentially large void, after the course ends and the close contacts to the students ceases quite abruptly. This is especially prevalent when the course focused on the challenges, where the users have their own expertise. The teachers have therefore initiated gathering of the participants on a few occasions after the course.

To conclude regarding the student outcome from the course, they expressed having a *new perspective on the users*, who they in the near future would meet in their own role as professionals. After the course, it is easier to see users' resources instead of only those challenges, which are the immediate occasion to the interaction between the user and the professional.

It is worth mentioning, that due to the first-time nature of this interdisciplinary gap-mending course, there were no academic credits given for this course. The students and users merely received a certificate describing the course content and the unique course framework. We find it extraordinary and uplifting that the students chose to spend 6 demanding weeks on this *extracurricular* course due to the unique opportunity to work alongside the users as equal partners. For many of the students, this course was completed parallel with their demanding bachelor studies.

In the context of the frequently held discussion on how to increase student motivation and study intensity, gap-mending courses seem to be one of the answers.

The veteran innovation course was from the outset planned as an important input to a large innovation camp, where knowledge might be shared, networking done and proposals generated for improving services offered to veterans with psychological injuries. Innovation camps were an integral part of the OPALL project, as a contribution to meet municipal welfare challenges.

Thus, on Metropolitan's initiative a full day *innovation camp* was held 4 months after completing the gap-mending course. The 60 participants came from user organisations, practitioners, local government authorities, private service providers, and some of the participating students and users from the course. The course findings and proposals were presented, and debated on an equal ground with the other proposals generated by the "professional" participants from experience. For the gap-mending course participants, this was a unique opportunity to be working as equals with the service providers, managers and NGOs.[12]

Following the positive evaluations of this gap-mending course by users, students and teachers, it was decided to plan a next user involving course.

---

12 Photos and resulting ideas from the innovation camp, including the ideas originating from the course, can be found here, in Danish: http://opall.dk/innovation _camp_veteraner. Cited: 2016-01-11.

This time, however, the course should be offered as an elective course on the last part of the study programmes, just before the bachelor thesis; and thus with full academic credits (10 ECTS) for the 6 week course. This new course would build on the veteran gap-mending course, but as we shall discuss in the following case, this time with some interesting alterations to the form and extent of involvement by both the users and the client.

Concept of the elective course "User involving innovation" masterclass

The course "User involving innovation" was offered to students at Metropolitan University College in the spring of 2015, again as a part of the R&D project, OPALL. The chosen welfare challenge was increasing inequality in health; also a theme that currently has large political and media attention.

This time the gap-mending course took on the role as facilitator of a unique cooperation between a local health authority (the client), 3 social housing associations (the partners), users from the social housing estates, and Metropolitan students and teachers.

The overall purpose of the course was to develop ideas for improved health services and initiatives, so more tenants from social housing estates are offered, attend and complete health promoting and disease prevention activities. The users were citizens with refugee and immigrant background from the three socially strained housing estates; this group representing up to 90 % of the tenants in these areas.[13]

Initially, the target user group were women, but in dialogue with the client and the partners, it was decided to also focus specifically on the male users. Men had generally proved to be more difficult to reach with traditional initiatives of health communication and related projects in the area in recent years. Better understanding of men as a target user group therefore was established as one criteria or one of the criteria of success for the course. Another criterion was that the users would find participation in the course meaningful.

The course was planned by an interdisciplinary Metropolitan team as later adjusted in collaboration with client, partners, and volunteers and key us-

---

13 Health was seen in a broader meaning, encompassing physical, mental and social well-being (in accordance with WHO definitions).

ers from the local housing association. The overall elements were as in the veteran gap-mending course.

Chronologically, due to the administrative routines concerning elective courses, the students had been recruited long before the client, partners and users. A small group of four Metropolitan students from Occupational Therapy, Physiotherapy and Nutrition and Health applied for the course, which made it possible to experiment with developing a masterclass-concept.

A central point in the course was to link theory and practice, while still ensuring a sufficient theoretical foundation. The students should both have the opportunity to make connections between theory and practice, and to be challenged theoretically. It was a concern that the courses should not develop into "practicism", or a pure model of apprenticeship. Critical, theoretical reflection and learning should be enhanced. For the this purpose the specific, theoretical "space" for reflection was developed: the "salons", where the four students, the teachers, a few selected Metropolitan employees, as well as the service providers, discussed relevant theoretical guest presentations, on equal grounds.

Within the dialogical approach of the course, elements of a model of apprenticeship were integrated. Here teachers act as role models for the students (Hiim/Hippe 2004), e.g. in working with the theoretical perspectives and in intense collaboration with users and service providers.

After recruiting the students and ensuring commitment from the client and partners, the users were to be recruited. In the process of establishing contact to users from the social housing estates, – specifically males with refugee or immigrant background – the Metropolitan team had valuable help from a key "gatekeeper" from one of the partnering housing associations. The message from the housing association representative to the team was clear:

> "Don't just come here presenting us with fancy academic talk (...) Go to the (men's) café, hang around. Just be there, get involved, talk to them, look what happens (...) Be there every Friday evening".

An introduction was thus made to some key male users: resourceful men in the area in charge of, among other things, a user-driven café, visited by the local men in general on Friday nights. It soon turned out that these men embraced this untraditional opportunity to discuss and develop health initiatives, and were thus willing to meet the teachers. Teachers from Metropolitan thereafter showed up at the user-driven café on Friday evenings in order to build a relationship and learn about the daily lives of the users. Appointments were also made to visit the women's café.

In the planning phase, some adjustments had already been made to the form of the user involvement. The user group was initially planned to be women with refugee or immigrant background, implying possible language barriers, limited educational backgrounds and often sole responsibility for young children. It was therefore not deemed realistic that the users should participate in an overnight future workshop in a rural setting, or in the salons, which were created to give room for more theoretical discussions. Instead the user involvement was planned to be focused on the four central workshops. The workshops were initially planned to take place during normal working hours and located at Metropolitan.

The process of making contact and recruiting users was a major learning experience, and caused several changes in the detailed planning and execution of the course as described in the following.

Realisation experiences of the elective masterclass

Development of trust and personal relations through the first, informal meetings in the male user café prior to the course start, played a key role in building up contact with a larger network of users, who proved eager to participate and contribute actively in the workshop courses. During the 5 week course, more than 40 users participated in the four workshops: Future, Prototype, Implementation Workshop and the Final, where the course proposals would be presented. As described below, the participation varied across the workshops.

Developing relations with users *prior* to the course was a crucial part of recruiting users for the workshops. The process was initiated by the teachers, and involved different stages. From the first somewhat awkward visits (in spite of a wholehearted welcome) in the men's café through developing recognition, a more relaxed atmosphere and closer ties were developed during the next visits.

The male users took the role of host very seriously and took full responsibility to introduce and show the teachers their environment and ensure support to the course. The contact was hereafter, as the course proceeded, slowly, "handed over" to the students, who found this a very motivating experience.

Following is a presentation of *key insights regarding the user participation* in the four workshops that were held during the course. A recurring feature was that service providers and users participated in all activities.

After meetings with service providers and some key users – and just before the course was about to start – it was decided that the workshops should be held separately for men and women respectively. Furthermore, the workshops should, if possible, be located in the users' cafés at times of day according to their daily activities.

Paying attention and *adjusting to the daily lives and needs of the users*, we were able to recruit more participants and achieve the highest level of active participation. The activities planned most flexibly likewise proved most successful.

The activities *located at the users' facilities* thus contributed to the participation of many users: At the future workshop for men, held Friday evening at 18:30 – 21:00 following mosque prayers, 27 men participated in the meeting room adjacent to their own user-driven café. An employee from the client also participated with great interest in this workshop, along with the students and the teachers.

The future workshop was planned with the least possible level of *structure*, containing only 4 key questions to discuss in groups. The contribution of the users was to give their views on: the theme of "Health"; their experiences and attitudes towards health promoting activities in their neighbourhoods; their own strategies for coping with health issues; and not least their needs, ideas and wishes for the future concerning their own health. These conversations were initiated with very basic questions about the users' needs and experiences. This low level of structure made it possible to pursue whichever points, statements or attitudes that appeared and take the dialogue in whatever direction the users found relevant.

We learned that activities characterized by higher levels of structure, planned in advance and without the possibility of changing plans after dialogue with practice, were more likely to face poorer participation; for example, prototyping, which had to be planned many weeks in advance because of the involvement of an external facilitator. In this instance, both the chosen time of day and location at Metropolitan later proved to cause fewer participants.

Having established a confidence-based relationship and by paying attention to the needs of the users when planning time and date, it was later possible to move some activities to Metropolitan. This was especially noticeable at the Final, which attracted many participants, especially – and quite unexpectedly – the men, who for the first time showed up at the Metropolitan premises. Location and timing of workshops, and the approach to recruitment of users is thus critical for the success of the courses.

Both during the course and in the evaluation of it, *the service provider* has acknowledged that the course was seen as representing a unique possibility to establish a collaboration of this kind: An institution of higher education represents a very welcome supply of resources to establish and develop contact with the users, where especially the male users have been difficult to reach for the service provider.

Some critical reflections regarding the gap-mending master class are shared below.

User involving courses make *ethical reflections* essential, e.g. the risk that the activities of the course are raising unrealistic expectations in users regarding their life situation. To which extent do users have the energy and necessary learning conditions to participate? Is it fair to ask them to participate in a "dream phase", if the user then expects the dreams to be implemented by the service provider the next month? Therefore a continuous discussion of the planned activities and balancing of expectations is necessary.

Evaluations highlighted that students during the course developed *new perspectives on the users*; they moved from viewing them as "disadvantaged", which is a conception often supported by e.g. the media, to developing a much more nuanced perspective, recognizing the many resources, the users actually proved to have. The students evaluated this as a very important learning outcome.

In the master class course it was, to a large extent, the meeting between the students and the users that took centre stage. This developed into a process that had a great impact on both parties who had an opportunity to learn and self-develop.

The users did not participate in all course activities but according to the *user-evaluations* at the final workshop of the course, they experienced empowerment through participation; experienced equality and discovered their own resources in the process of being co-creators who were listened to and taken into account. On many occasions, the users expressed gratitude for being invited to share their views and ideas, "on their own terms", as they stated it.

The gap-mending course conducted as a master class has had a clear, *relevant and motivating link between theory and practice*. It has also been a complex construction involving many "masters": teachers, service providers and users. At times it has proved a difficult balancing act for teachers, students, users and service providers, each having their own expectations of the course, and each their assessment of the relevance of the proposals developed. Early action towards role clarification and continued balancing of expectations is crucial in order to stay focused on the needs of the users and how to develop solutions. This requires much closer communication with all involved than traditional courses imply.

In effect, this form of more experimental user-involving learning activities *demand specific competencies of both the teachers and the students* participating: Teachers must be willing to enter into new relationships with users and an unusually close relation with the students, providing a maximum of support and working very consciously to facilitate the process for the students.

Students must be willing to challenge themselves to a maximum and accept a high level of uncertainty and flexibility. In return, they have participated in a course that has facilitated their development of competencies and prepared them to participate in a complex practice, demanding innovative, interdisciplinary, and user-empowering competencies.

Finally, in this gap-mending course there were also post-course implementation initiatives. The intense involvement throughout the course had the users pushing towards the realisation of their ideas. At the end of the course, a pilot project could thus be announced starting less than two months later. Based directly on the suggestions and adaptations from the course, the pilot consisted of a health café in the largest of the social housing areas, where men and women could drop by for a health check and counselling on relevant health subjects in an informal atmosphere. The service was offered by the course client, the municipal health authority, together with Metropolitan students from the nursing and occupational therapy field. Following the project, Metropolitan continues to conduct these health checks monthly, giving the involved students a unique chance to meet users in their own environment and practice communication and health care skills.

Evaluations and critical reflections

Gap-mending courses come in many colours; we have shared experiences from two of the courses carried out at Metropolitan University College.

In both these courses, the intended emphasis has been on user involvement in practice development rather than user involvement in education. This was due to the courses evolving as part of a large partnership project with the overall aim of practice development, cf. solving municipal welfare challenges. In our courses, the users have therefore been included as equal partners, working towards the joint goal of developing new ideas for improving social work and other welfare practices. Thus, inclusion in a common learning experience has been a very positive side effect rather than the goal itself. The focus on a specific common objective brings students and users to focus on their contributions to better future practice, regardless of whether they are users or students.

User involving courses <u>are</u> more time-consuming for both teachers and students, compared to traditional courses. As has been discussed in both cases, the students are under more pressure, due to more complex learning situations demanding flexibility, close dialogue, and cooperation with the users and the teachers especially, and to a lesser extent also with the service providers. This places high demands on the students' ability to cope with uncertainty as well as their ability to communicate and collaborate with course colleagues from different backgrounds, whether users or students from other disciplines.

This however, is the true benefit of the gap-mending courses. They have provided the students an opportunity to not only learn *about* the subject through theoretical studies; rather, the students have experienced user involvement first hand, and had the chance to train and practise user empowerment and development of practice.

There is a considerable pedagogical potential in this close connection and cooperation with practice, as the learning processes build upon the students solving "real" problems in cooperation with service providers and users. This type of close cooperation furthers the chance of the proposals being implemented and tested in a real practice setting, potentially leading to a change of practice. For the students, these courses are thus an opportunity become an active co-creator of the field of practice in which they will find future occupation shortly after the course. This was where the real theory-practice transfer took place.

In a further educational context, student evaluations implied that user involving courses seemed to have a noticeable effect on students' motivation, active participation and commitment: Commitment to the users, who are met as individuals, with life stories of their own, personal narratives and resources perhaps undiscovered. The students also expressed a large commitment to fellow students in the interprofessional collaborative practice. A major learning outcome was thus in the shape of greater clarity about their own professional competencies.

We found that inviting service providers as clients, taking an active role in communicating or implementing some of the course proposals, certainly increases the chance of making an impact beyond the duration of the course. In this respect, it is a challenge if resources are not committed to support post-course implementation of some of the most promising proposals. Being integrated as part of R&D projects was a chance to find these extra resources. In this way, the high user expectations resulting from the participation in the course, could to some extent be met, as they saw some of their proposals implemented.

We have been true to the PowerUs statement: "Gap-mending methods calls for as equal grounds as possible in the mutual learning situation" (PowerUs 2013: 3). This involves adjusting the learning situation to encompass the users. In the gap-mending course, where the users were social housing tenants with refugee or immigrant background, this led to some adjustments in location, timing and form of the activities: The critical learning activities and workshops were moved out of the classroom and into the meeting rooms of the users' social housing areas; some workshops where scheduled for Friday evenings after mosque gatherings, and some learning situations were held in parallel sessions for male and women users, reflecting their daily practices in their neighborhood activities, whereas students were mixed gender.

In the gap-mending courses described, each course focused on one specific social practice challenge and one overall user group. This entails an opportunity to work more focused on developing improved practice. We also found it provided a valuable opportunity to adjust the courses to the given user group, in order to make the common learning situation as equal as possible. The advantage is empowerment of the users, who stand on a firmer – more equal – platform. The adjustments to create as equal grounds as possible, also provides a unique extra learning experience for the students: They gain an insight into how to meet the users on equal terms – and thus as perhaps more resourceful users – in their future jobs as welfare workers.

At Metropolitan, the initial R&D project, which fostered the two gap-mending courses described in this chapter, has been completed. However, in the true spirit of gap-mending, our experiences, evaluations and recommendations are currently being passed on to teaching colleagues at Metropolitan, who are responsible for new 10-week, interdisciplinary and non-elective courses: "Developing welfare together – locally". While the first generation of these courses are with users in the traditional role as informants, we are confident that more gap-mending elements will be included in the next generation of the courses – inviting the users in as co-creators, on equal ground.

References

Bason, Christian (2010): *"Leading public sector innovation: Co-creation for a better society"* Bristol: Policy Press.

Barr, Hugh/Low, Helena. (2013): *Introducing Interprofessional Education.* Fareham: CAIPE.

Centre For The Advancement Of Interprofessional Education (CAIPE) (2002): *Defining Interprofessional Education.* Retrieved on 22.01.2016 from: http://caipe.org.uk/about-us/defining-ipe/.

Hiim, Hilde/Hippe, Else. (2004): *Undervisningsplanlægning for faglærere [Didactics for professionals* (2. udgave). Copenhagen: Gyldendals Lærerbibliotek.

Lauvås, Kirsti/Lauvås, Per (2010): *"Tværfagligt samarbejde – Perspektiv og strategi" [Interdisciplinary collaborative practice – perspectives and strategies]* Aarhus: KLIM.

PowerUS (2013): "Mend The Gap. Co-learning methods for a mobilising social work" Retrieved on 22.01.2016 from: http://powerus.se/wp-content/uploads/PowerUs Brochure_2013.pdf%20.

Uddannelses- og Forskningsudvalget (2014): *"Uddannelsesfremsyn på sundhedsområdet" [Educational foresight in the health care sector.]*, Copenhagen: Uddannelses- og Forskningsministeriet (Ministry of Higher Education and Science).

3.5 Germany: Service User Involvement at Esslingen University of Applied Sciences: Background, Concept and Experiences

Thomas Heidenreich and Marion Laging

This chapter presents the development, implementation and evaluation of a series of Service User Involvement (SUI) seminars at Esslingen University of Applied Sciences. We will briefly describe the modalities of social work education in Germany as a whole and in Esslingen in particular and will present some of the challenges in implementing SUI seminars into an existing curriculum. The series of SUI seminars at Esslingen is described in some detail as well as the evaluations given by both student and user participants. Furthermore, we will present our conclusions with regard to the effects and possibilities of SUI as well as remaining questions and future perspectives.

Context of the course

Social work as an academic discipline has – at least compared to other disciplines – a relatively short history in Germany (Kuhlmann 2013). After their early history as colleges without university status, schools of social work underwent a process of professional development by being changed into universities of applied sciences in the 1960s, and were thus incorporated into the tertiary educational system. Virtually all social work courses in Germany have by now undergone the Bologna process and have thus been changed from diploma to bachelor's/master's courses. The curricula of social work programmes in Germany vary in a number of ways. However, there are a large number of similarities between universities and constant discussions in the *Fachbereichstag Soziale Arbeit* (National Association of Schools of Social Work), the German national assembly of deans of social work faculties/departments involved in teaching social work. The National Association of Schools of Social Work brings together professional, organisational and educational policy-related activities from around 80 locations including universities of applied sciences, former comprehensive universities/ polytechnics, which now have the status of universities (e.g. Kassel), and the church-funded and managed universities (cf. http://www.fbts.de/. Cited: 2016-01-11).

The "Qualification Framework for Social Work" (*QFSW, Qualifikationsrahmen Soziale Arbeit*) edited by the National Association of Schools of Social Work defines the qualifications that social work education in Germany is supposed to teach at bachelor, master and PhD levels. The qualifications to be obtained during studies are divided into six different areas (see Table 1). As can be seen, there is a strong emphasis on academic content (which is quite typical for German social work, according to Kruse (2004) and Hamburger (2015)) and there are no points specifically related to contact with service users.

These areas are further specified using operational criteria for BA, MA and PhD levels. A consideration of SUI approaches against the elements of the qualification frame reveals that SUI is potentially relevant for all areas mentioned in the qualification framework (see above – Introduction): e.g. service users could be involved in the planning and conception of social work (QFSW area C), in the organisation, performance and evaluation of social work (QFSW area E) as well as in research (QFSW area D).

Table 1: Areas of qualification according to the Qualification Framework for Social Work

A. Knowledge and Understanding/Comprehension
B. Description, Analysis and Evaluation
C. Planning and Conception of Social Work
D. Search and Research in Social Work
E. Organisation, Performance and Evaluation in Social Work
F. Professional General Abilities and Attitudes in Social Work
G. Personal Characteristics and Attitudes

Source: Bartosch et al., 2008 (emphasis: the authors), http://www.fbts.de/fileadmin/fbts/Dokumente/QRSArb_englisch_5.1.pdf. Cited: 2016-01-11.

However, as SUI approaches are new to Germany, service user involvement in the teaching of competencies in these areas is virtually non-existent (but poses interesting perspectives for the future). Of course, this does not mean that service users have not had any involvement in social work education in Germany until now; on the contrary, there are numerous examples of service users being invited to discuss their personal history and their experiences with the helping system. Rather, the innovative point is that a coherent conceptual framework is emerging in which service users find their place in social work education and SUI is considered a quality characteristic of training across an international framework.

For the implementation of SUI approaches into individual BA-level courses, the QFSW areas F and G ("Professional general abilities and attitudes in social work" and "Personal characteristics and attitudes") are of special interest: at the BA level, the qualification framework requires a *"strong ability to communicate and interact with all professional and non-professional actors in the field as well as in their context in society"* (Domain F, BA level, Item 2). Domain F, BA level, Item 4 states as one of the aims of social work education *"the ability to recognize and to weigh the interests of clients, client groups or systems"*. We expect that SUI seminars, while no doubt conveying information on the areas A to E, can be especially relevant for the contents of areas F and G. While the basics of most of these areas can be learned in an academic setting, practice and application of this knowledge are very important. This need for "hands-on" experience is usually taken care of by including experiential teaching elements such as visiting different professional areas of social work and having students complete an internship semester (30 ECTS) in one of these settings.

In spite of this widely acknowledged need for practical experience, there has been heated debate about the role practice should play in social work education (Kruse 2004: 118) with strong arguments in favor of a more theoretical approach which would, in turn, strengthen the academic character of social work. In this climate, involving service users or organisations of service users such as self-help groups in social work education is not a priority. Nevertheless, in the German health and social care systems, self-help groups are well established: it is estimated that there are more than 280 administrative centers under professional leadership with the sole aim of supporting self-help groups. Each of these administrative centers serves on average 180 individual self-help groups. (http://www.nakos.de/data/Fachpublikationen/2015/DAGSHG-Jahrbuch-15-Nickel-ua.pdf. Cited: 2016-01-11). However, most of these self-help groups do not have a strong political emphasis in their work but are rather intended to help people cope with their respective conditions or problems.

Including service user involvement elements in the curriculum of a German faculty of social work needs careful planning (indeed, we are aware of a review paper that describes the "participatory turn" in British social work (Leers/Rieger 2013) in the German language but, to our knowledge, no papers describing SUI projects in Germany have been published yet): all bachelor's and master's programs in Germany are accredited on a regular basis by accreditation agencies and each department has to make sure that they follow the procedures formulated in the "Module Handbook", which specifies contexts, workload and other aspects of each module taught in the course of social work training. Implementing a service user involvement seminar can thus follow two different routes: 1. setting up a new module that is specifically designed as an SUI seminar (which makes a change to the module handbook necessary), or 2. implementing the SUI seminar within an existing module in the curriculum. As route 1 typically takes a long time to implement, we chose route 2 by organizing the module "student project" as an SUI seminar at our department of social work. To illustrate this process, we will briefly introduce our department and the structure of the curriculum of the BA course in social work. We will then describe how we implemented an SUI seminar within this seminar.

Outline of the course

Located near Stuttgart in the south of Germany, Esslingen University of Applied Sciences offers a bachelor's degree course (7 semesters, 210 ECTS) as well as a master's degree course (3 semesters, 90 ECTS) in social work with an intake of 93 students per semester in the bachelor's course and 35 students per year in the master's course. We decided to integrate the SUI seminar into the BA-level course as we found a high level of congruence between the professional competencies described for the BA level in the qualification framework introduced above (Professional general abilities and attitudes in social work, Personal Characteristics and Attitudes) and the aims of SUI programs. This does not imply, however, that we consider QFSW areas F and G the only reasonable targets for SUI approaches at the BA level; rather, this can be thought of as an initial step. The decision to implement an SUI course in Esslingen was inspired by earlier work by the PowerUs network (PowerUs 2013).

Curriculum of the BA in Social Work in Esslingen

To understand the context in which the SUI seminar was implemented, it is necessary to give a brief overview of the curriculum: students obtain 210 ECTS over the course of 7 semesters with one semester (usually the fourth) as an internship of at least 100 days in a social work setting. The first two semesters form the first part of the course (with a heavy emphasis on basic knowledge), while the third to the seventh semesters form the second part of course[14]. The contents are organized into six study areas: (I. Societal context of social work; II. Individuals and groups within their living environment; III. Organizational framework of social work; IV. Social work as a profession; V. Social work as a science and discipline; and VI. Social work as an area of intervention. A number of different modes of teaching are also employed, including lectures, seminars, internships with accompanying theory-practice seminars.

One of the elements in area VI ("intervention"), an elective course, seemed especially suitable for implementing an SUI approach: the "project seminar" which is taught during the 5th and 6th semester and thus spans a whole year and carries 16 ECTS. According to the module handbook, the aim of the project seminar is to draw on the experiences gained during the intern-

---

14 The Module Handbook can be downloaded – in English language – http://www.hs-esslingen.de/fileadmin/medien/fakultaeten/sp/Formulare/Fuer_Studierende/English_module_descriptions_BSA.pdf). Cited: 2016-01-11.

ship in the fourth semester and the theoretical content of the earlier semesters by initiating a project that brings together theory and practice. More specifically, students are expected to plan, conduct and evaluate a joint enterprise based in an area of social work, and combining elements of theory and practice. This module offers ample opportunities for both teachers and students (and, in this case, service users) to design a project that is in line with basic ideas of SUI and which can be understood as an attempt to "mend the gap". The concept of "gap-mending" was introduced by the PowerUs network (PowerUs 2013) which emphasised the importance of bridging discrepancies between theoretical knowledge and the experiential knowledge of service users. Other areas where gap-mending seems especially relevant are gaps between the professional role and the person of the helper, gaps between professionals and clients and also between teachers and students.

Description of the "project seminars" designed to develop, implement and evaluate SUI seminars

At the time of preparing this book chapter, two project seminars (one of which started in March 2014, the other in March 2015) had been conducted. Both of these project seminars organised SUI seminars that will be described in more detail below.

The first group of eight students decided to start working on the SUI idea (**project seminar I**) in March 2014. As is typical for this module, the lecturers (the authors) provided a framework while the specific modalities of the SUI seminar were developed collaboratively. During the first sessions of the seminar, students read widely on SUI projects across Europe (e.g. Askheim 2011; Kjellberg 2011; Stevens/Tanner 2006) and discussed their applicability within the current setting. Several areas central to the concept of SUI were identified and discussed in great detail (e.g. "empowerment" and "participation"). One central topic that emerged from these discussions was the question "What is good social work?" or more precisely: which aspects of users' experiences with social work and social workers are/were helpful and which were not. These questions and the idea to produce a DVD were inspired by the work of Helen Casey (see Chapter 3.3) and her Durham team as a member of the PowerUs Network; they interviewed children and adolescents who were currently involved with social workers. In a process detailed by Laging and Heidenreich (submitted for publication) the specific format of the SUI seminar (SUI seminar I) was influenced by discussions with both professionals and self-help groups. Our experiences in approaching potential participants for our SUI seminars will be detailed in the next section.

Project seminar II was comprised of 18 students, started in March 2015 and followed the same course format as project seminar I: again, students familiarised themselves with different SUI concepts across Europe. Additionally, they watched the DVD produced during the course of **project seminar I** and had the opportunity to discuss experiences with students who had participated in the earlier seminar. As **project seminar I** had gathered some evidence on topics that might be interesting for both students and service users, it was decided to focus on the dialectic of "help vs. control" which is central to conducting social work, especially in highly regulated settings such as help for probationers or people with mental health problems involving suicidal tendencies. To select participants, it was decided to continue working with the groups that had already successfully participated in **SUI seminar I** while at the same time aiming to involve more groups (see next section for more details). As a next step, students checked where service user involvement would be most appropriate in the social work bachelor's curriculum. After identifying relevant modules, the student group approached professors who teach in these modules and personally discussed possibilities for incorporating SUI in these modules. Most professors were open with regard to including service users in teaching social work. Finally, near the end of **project seminar II**, the students organized a meeting where service users and professors met (see next section) to discuss possible ways of collaboration.

Approaching service users for SUI projects

Across Europe, different service user groups have already been included in SUI seminars (e.g. users of mental health services, people who grew up in care). Initially, we had no constraints as to which service users to include in our seminar. Rather, we chose a participatory approach in which students were encouraged to consider working with the service user groups they were especially interested in. Also, we were interested in finding out about service user organisations which were open to involving themselves with university settings. As can be expected, the students' interests varied widely, often according to experiences gained in previous internships. Stemming from these experiences, some students had access to service user populations they were familiar with. However, in Germany (and probably in most other countries) user groups vary to a large degree as to how strongly they are "organised": while there are some groups that have developed elaborate structures of user organisation, other groups are either not organised at all or organised by other parties. Some well-organised groups can be found in mental health settings and in the field of addictions: one of the structured approaches in mental health settings is called *Experts by Experience* (EX-IN) where people who have experienced (treatment in) mental health services are trained to take the role of a peer who helps others in the process of recovery, thus gaining insights into their own problems (Jahnke 2012; Utschakowski/Sielaff/Bock/ Winter 2016). EX-IN is a comprehensive training programme that aims at opening up new vocational and personal perspectives for people with experiences of psychiatric treatment. Experiences with mental crises and psychiatric services are discussed and reflected on in these courses and they form the foundation for work as a recovery companion and/or lecturer. Of special importance is that the EX-IN program also prepares members for teaching activities: EX-IN graduates are aware that their personal and reflected history may be important for others in teaching situations and for educational aims. Thus, graduates of EX-IN courses are very well prepared to participate in SUI seminars. Esslingen University of Applied Sciences has mentored the set-up of these EX-IN courses as well as their implementation from the very start and has very good relationships with their organisers. These courses exist in a large number of federal states in Germany. In Baden-Wuerttemberg (the federal state where Esslingen is located) there is the special situation that the EX-IN course is run by a self-help group of persons with experience of the psychiatric system. In the field of addiction, there is a large number of self-help groups in Germany (as well as in other countries), some of which use the twelve-step format. Though meetings take place in small groups, the groups are also organized at state and national levels (e.g. the "Circles of Friends" (*Freundeskreise*) in the Esslingen area). In comparison, members of non-organised groups are very hard to approach. Thus, in a participatory process with the students, it was decided for **SUI seminar I** to focus on persons with experience of mental health services and on persons with an addiction who are already organized. One further aim was to develop methods for getting into contact with participants from other groups which are less organized and less prepared for SUI.

With regard to the selection of participants, Project **seminar II** drew heavily on experiences gained during **Project seminar I** and **SUI seminar I**:

it was decided early on that the successful work initiated with mental health and addiction groups would be continued (although with a new focus) while at the same time new groups should be included. Work with the EX-IN group was specifically focused on continuing the successful work started in **Project seminar I** and thereby provided continuity in an ongoing collaboration with this group. The students of this group had the aim of carving out what a broader, more sustainable and more systematic way of including service users in the BA social work course in Esslingen could look like (over and above the project seminar initiated by the authors). Further, they intended to start with implementing these ideas. Given these aims, collaboration with EX-IN graduates seemed especially promising because some EX-IN graduates had already participated in SUI seminar I and especially in filming the DVD; our experience showed that SUI approaches and the philosophy of EX-IN proved to be highly compatible.

Due to the specific interests and experiences of students who participated in **Project seminar II**, two new groups were added: 1. former prisoners who were still on probation and under supervision by social workers, and 2. young parents living in a parent-child facility who had experience with youth welfare services. In the context of project seminar II, three SUI seminars were developed, conducted and evaluated: **SUI seminar II.1** was organised for patients with experience of mental health services, **SUI seminar II.2** was for people with an addiction and people on probation, while **SUI seminar II.3** was conducted for parents living in a parent-child facility. Table 2 shows an overview of project seminars and the service user involvement seminars that were developed in this context.

Table 2: Overview of project seminars and SUI seminars conducted at Esslingen University of Applied Sciences

Project seminar	Time	SUI seminars	SU group
Project seminar I	March 2014-January 2015	SUI seminar I	Mental health experiences, addiction
Project seminar II	March 2015-January 2016	SUI seminar II.1	Mental health experiences
		SUI seminar II.2	Addictions/probation
		SUI seminar II.3	Families

SUI service user involvement, SU service user

Realisation, implementation and experiences

In this book chapter, due to constraints on space, we will describe two of the SUI seminars in some detail (**SUI seminar I** and **SUI seminar II.1**), while only briefly introducing SUI seminars II.2 and II.3. Both SUI seminar I and SUI seminar II.1 worked with the same group of service users (persons with experience of the mental health system) and SUI seminar II.1 constituted a logical continuation of elements from SUI seminar I.

Service user involvement seminar I

The conceptualisation of **SUI seminar I** was done collaboratively between the two lecturers (the authors) and the student group of 8 students using input from professionals (a platform called "regional practice") and service users. During these discussions it became clear that organising the seminar as a week-long meeting was impossible: the user groups comprised unemployed people as well as people with regular working hours and for the latter it was judged to be highly unlikely that they would use their holiday time for the seminar. Thus, the seminar was organised as a weekend seminar (Saturday and Sunday) and a follow-up meeting (workday evening). Service users received compensation for participation. Nine service users (from the field of mental health services and addictions) agreed to participate. The main question discussed at the weekend – using a variety of different methods – was "What is good social work?" Table 3 shows the sequence of elements implemented during the weekend and the follow-up meeting. Wherever possible, service users, students and professors entered the discussions on an equal footing, e.g. when discussing experiences with social work, all groups were encouraged to report on their personal experiences. While a large number of qualities required by social workers were mentioned and discussed, the professional relationship of social workers and their clients was described as the most important topic. Other elements included informing service users about the format of the BA course in social work at Esslingen – this helped service users to experience students as "just ordinary people" who gain knowledge in this specific area. One key element of SUI seminar I was the production of a DVD in which service users were able to report on their positive and negative experiences with social work as well as formulate expectations for future generations of social workers.

Table 3: Contents and methods of SUI seminar I

Contents	Methods
Day 1	
Warming-up	Postcards, guided introductions, experience with social work
Empowerment	Input – definition of empowerment
	Experience-based sharing of experiences
	Meaning of empowerment for myself
BA course social work in Esslingen	Input by students, discussion
Personal experiences with social work	World café using different triggers, e.g. Where did I experience social work? What helped me? What hurt me? How should social workers act?
Day 2	
Wishes for social work? What should SW look like in the future?	Work in pairs: student – service user
	Plenary discussion
Reflection	Discussion: What was important for me during the weekend?
Filming	
Conclusion and feedback	Guided plenary discussion: impressions, ideas for extensions,
Follow-Up Meeting	
Introduction and DVD	Watching the DVD produced during the weekend and discussion
Farewell and further collaboration	

At the follow-up meeting shown in table 3, service users, students and teachers came together once more to watch and discuss the DVD produced at the workshop. Service users were enthusiastic about the content and quality of the film and felt that their aims in conveying their needs were well met.

Service user involvement seminar II.1

For SUI seminar II.1, the students invited EX-IN graduates for a workshop at Esslingen University to find out about the conditions, wishes, requirements and worries of service users with regard to collaborating in the BA course in social work. One central result of this workshop was that there are a large number of conditions that are particular for each participant. On the one hand, there are a number of formal requirements, e.g. size of student group and possible times. Additionally, there are some requirements related to the content of the course, e.g. choice of topics that can be discussed. One condition that was important for all EX-IN graduates was that there should be adequate compensation for service users who participate in seminars. EX-IN graduates further emphasised that they need an individual and reliable contact person from the teaching staff with whom they can discuss the setting, the aims and the contents of the session(s) in which they are going to participate. It should be kept in mind that even though service users are highly motivated to take part in social work education (and in this case even have special training), the stresses and strains they may experience in their daily lives necessitate careful planning so that the experience is not overwhelming.

At the end of this project, another workshop ("matching meeting") was conducted in which service users and professors that were interested in involving service users could meet and discuss opportunities for collaboration. As a product of this project, students created index cards with individual profiles of users detailing interests and experiences for further collaboration with professors. Additionally, we are currently working on a Facebook page which is designed to simplify communication between the University and service users (e.g. posting interesting events). These are the first steps to anchor SUI in social work education in Esslingen in a broader and more systematic way.

Service user involvement seminars II.2 and II.3

The two SUI seminars that will only be mentioned briefly ventured into new areas for possible service user involvement: one student group was especially interested in people who had been in prison and were still on probation. By approaching social workers who work in this field, they were able to establish contact with service users from this area. The SUI seminar was run over a weekend and was mainly concerned with the effects of stigma and discrimination. Both service users and students found the discussions very relevant and interesting. As one service user commented: "Until now, I was not aware of being discriminated against".

SUI seminar II.3 was organised for parents who had got into difficulties while raising their young children; it consisted of mostly single mothers (and one single father) who lived in an institution near Esslingen. The students decided to broach the issue of "help vs control". In this context, this dialectical pair of nouns describes a typical role conflict of social workers: while on the one hand, they have a special remit to make sure that the children are not harmed, on the other they are also involved in a personal helping process. SUI seminar II.3 met at two different times: first for an evening-long introduction into the themes and then for a half-day workshop where these issues were discussed.

Evaluations and critical reflections

All the activities reported so far were carefully evaluated using different methodological approaches. We will first report on service user and student feedback for project seminar I and SUI seminar I before discussing project seminar II and SUI seminar II. We will then evaluate and critically reflect on our approach to SUI and will discuss implications for the future.

Evaluation of project seminar I and SUI seminar I

To evaluate project seminar I and SUI seminar I, both service users and students were asked for feedback immediately after the workshop. The service users' comments in a semi-structured interview were analysed using qualitative methods. Both methods and results of this study are detailed in Laging and Heidenreich (submitted for publication) and will only be briefly summarised here: the service users' responses were coded using MAXQDA. A number of major categories could be identified: (1) importance of exchange with students, gaining new perspectives; (2) knowledge about social work theories; (3) practice experience, e.g. getting to know other service users; (4) personal benefits from the seminar; (5) experiencing a university setting; and (6) future expectations, especially the hope that this newly formed collaboration should continue. The results confirmed that all the service users that were interviewed responded positively.

The students' feedback on the seminar and also the whole project was positive (see also Laging/Heidenreich, submitted for publication): most of all, the students valued having the opportunity to get into direct contact with service users. One special effect of this contact was diminished anxiety when anticipating working with service users in the future. Several students pointed out that they were impressed with what service users told them about the course of their lives and the obstacles they had to overcome. It became clear that students reported feeling more connected to service users after the seminar.

Evaluation of project seminar II/SUI seminar II.1

The aim of this project was to find out in which ways service users could be involved in social work education. For this aim, service users, students and teachers were brought together. One very important result of this project was that personally "matching" service users and teachers is important for SUI to succeed. To find possible matches, a large amount of information, discussions and preliminary work is necessary. Some initial elements of a systematic cooperative structure were developed in Esslingen, e.g. by developing the system of index cards.

Furthermore, students were very intrinsically motivated to enable a broader and more systematic inclusion of service users in social work education. This student interest also helped teachers to get interested in SUI. On the other hand, experience showed that participation – here the participation of students in shaping their lessons – mobilised extraordinary resources of energy and new developments. For further developments in SUI, including students more systematically should also be considered.

General evaluation

After two one-year user involvement seminars with a total of 26 students and more than 30 service users in the course of the Esslingen BA Social Work curriculum, our evaluation is very positive: students, teachers and recipients of social work experienced large benefits from the SUI seminars. Starting from international contacts and the impressive projects in other European countries, we wanted to test the SUI approach in the German system. We found out that the basic idea received very good feedback, first from students and later from colleagues. This might also be due to the fact that participation plays a major role in the theory and practice of social work in Germany (e.g. Oelerich/Schaarschuch 2005). Esslingen University also has a record of participatory collaboration with students – thus, including service users into social work education appeared to be a logical consequence of known theories and well-tried practical approaches.

Having said that, it also became clear that specific adaptations to the requirements and conditions of each country and university are necessary:

The projects in Lund (Sweden) and Lillehammer (Norway) involve service users mainly as "external students", thereby giving them a role that emphasises meetings between internal students and service users as equals.

During the developmental process at Esslingen, a slightly different structure emerged: the students became – at least in part – organizers and designers of Service User Involvement seminars and the participants who had graduated from EX-IN seminars aimed at a role as lecturer, a position within the academic system that is on an equal level with academic teachers. In this way, in Esslingen – as in other projects in Europe – new role patterns and levels of encounter emerged, although in a slightly different way.

Critical reflection

Besides all the positive aspects discussed above, we are aware that the work done on service user involvement in our department is only a starting point: coming back to the qualification framework of social work introduced above, there are a large number of areas for possible service user involvement which we have not yet addressed. Future work might find a role for service users in the other areas such as "knowledge and understanding" and especially "description, analysis and evaluation": service users could be involved in defining criteria to evaluate successful social work. Service users could also be involved in planning and conceptualization, research and organisation. One interesting, related question is "What are the motives of service users for participating in SUI projects?" (see Grant 2012). When deciding where to include SUI in our social work course, we chose the area of intervention as a starting point. Looking back, this decision seems reasonable. However, there are other areas where

SUI approaches might enrich teaching: e.g. the area "Societal context of social work" might benefit from SUI, e.g. by service users, teachers and students working on sociological themes such as poverty which frequently befalls service users (see Gupta/Blevitt 2008). Similarly, service users might participate in shaping the organisational framework of social work and also in defining scientifically relevant areas of research. SUI approaches will be continued at our university in a variety of ways: we intend to keep collaborating with individual service users and service user organizations such as EX-IN and the "Friends of People with Addictions" (*Freundeskreise Suchtkrankenhilfe*). Indeed, there are plans to take collaboration to a higher level by initiating contact with organisations on a federal and national level. On the other hand, we intend to bring SUI approaches to a variety of service user groups not yet involved, such as children in care settings, refugees and older people. Another aim is to anchor SUI approaches more deeply in the faculty – initial discussions with colleagues have been positive. We will draw inspiration from sources such as Advocacy in Action (2006) and Askheim (2011) as well as Baldwin and Sadd (2006). Other perspectives include developing new ways of assessment for students, such as role-plays to assess readiness for practice (Skilton 2011; Duffy/Das/Davidson 2013), an approach that is also used in medical education.

We conclude that even though we were able to gain significant new insights and initiate some interesting developments, some questions remain. On a conceptual level, as briefly discussed in Laging and Heidenreich (submitted), a broader inclusion of SUI principles in the faculty (e.g. in other areas of the BA curriculum) raises a number of questions that need answering before SUI principles can be realised in more depth. One of these questions is the possible role of service users in academic areas such as examinations (as in Great Britain). Also, empowering service users to participate in social work education as equals will be an important issue because, after their experiences with hierarchical structures, discussions with professionals on an equal footing can problematic. Also, even though our first impressions were very positive, it cannot be ruled out that there might be negative effects of SUI: e.g. vulnerable service users might be stressed by interactions with students, while students might find difficulties in maintaining a professional role. More research is needed to find answers to these questions. More specifically, studies should be initiated that evaluate the effects of SUI projects on a number of dimensions, such as students' attitudes towards service users and vice versa. Also, it should be made sure that service users are able to attend meetings at regional, national and international levels; while professors can usually get funding for traveling to international conferences, service users are very often financially challenged, thus making it impossible to attend meetings without special funding. Finally, we are in the process of introducing SUI approaches into the German professional discussion (Laging/Heidenreich 2016).

References

Advocacy In Action with Staff/Students from the University of Nottingham (2006): *Making It Our Own Ball Game: Learning and Assessment in Social Work Education*. Social Work Education, Vol. 25, No. 4, pp. 332-346.

Askheim, Ole P. (2011): *'Meeting Face to Face Creates New Insights': Recruiting Persons with User Experiences as Students in an Educational Programme in Social Work*. Social Work Education, First Article, pp. 1-13.

Baldwin, Mark/Sadd, June (2006): *Allies with Attitude! Service Users, Academics and Social Service Agency Staff Learning How to Share Power in Running Social Work Education Courses*. Social Work Education, Vol. 25, No. 4, pp. 348-359.

Bartosch, Ulrich/Maile, Anita/Speth, Christine (2008). Qualifikationsrahmen Soziale Arbeit (QR SArb). *[Qualification Framework Social Work]*.Version 5.1. available at: http://www.fbts.de/fileadmin/fbts/Aktuelles/QRSArb_Version_5.1.pdf, last download January 8th, 2016.

Duffy, Joe/Das, Chaitali/Davidson, Gavin (2013): *Service User and Carer Involvement in Role-plays to Assess Readiness for Practice*. Social Work Education, Vol. 32, No. 1, pp. 39-54.

Gant, Valerie (2012): *An exploration of the motivations of service users and carers involved in student social work education and the challenges that such involvement brings*. Enhancing the Learner Experience in Higher Education, Vol. 4, No. 1, pp. 44-58.

Gupta, Anna/Blewett, James (2008): *Involving Services Users in Social Work Training on the Reality of Family Poverty: A Case Study of a Collaborative Project*. Social Work Education, Vol. 27, No. 5, pp. 459-473.

Hamburger, Franz/Hirschler, Sandra/Sander, Günther/Wöbcke, Manfred (2015). Ausbildung für Soziale Arbeit in Europa.[Education for Social Work in Europe] In: Otto / Thiersch (Hg.). Handbuch Soziale Arbeit. München: Ernst Reinhardt, GmbH & Co KG, pp. 123-130.

Jahnke, Bettina (2012). Vom Ich-Wissen zum Wir-Wissen: Mit EX-IN zum Genesungsbegleiter. *[From I-knowledge to We-knowledge: becoming a recovery companion with EX-IN]*. Neumünster: Die Brücke.

Kjellberg, Gun/French, Robert (2012): *A New Pedagogical Approach for Integrating Social Work Students and Service Users*. Social Work Education, Vol. 30, No. 8, pp. 947-963.

Kruse, Elke (2004). Stufen zur Akademisierung. Wege der Ausbildung für Soziale Arbeit von der Wohlfahrtsschule zum Bachelor-/Mastermodell. [Steps toward academisation. Ways of social work education from the welfare school to the Bachelor/Master model] Wiesbaden: VS-Verlag.

Kuhlmann, Carola (2013): Geschichte Sozialer Arbeit, Band 1: Studienbuch. [*History of Social Work, Part 1: study book*].Schwalbach: Wochenschau-Verlag.

Laging, Marion/Heidenreich, Thomas (submitted for publication): Service User Involvement in Social Work Education: Experiences from Germany and Implications for a European Perspective. *European Journal of Social Work.*

Laging, Marion/Heidenreich, Thomas (2016): Was ist gute Soziale Arbeit? *StudentInnen und Service User arbeiten gemeinsam in einem Lehr- und Lernprojekt.* [What is good social work? Students and service users work together in a teaching and learning project]. *Sozial Extra, 2/2016, 10-13,* DOI 10.1007/s12054-015-0021-4.

Leers, Franziska A./Rieger, Judith: *Erfahrungsbasierte Lehre und andere Formen des Service User Involvements als Ausdruck der partizipativen Wende in der Hochschulbildung im Studiengang Soziale Arbeit in England.* [*Experience-based learning and other forms of service user involvement as indicator of the participatory turn in programs of social work in England*]. Neue Praxis, 06/2013, pp. 537-550.

Oelerich, Gertrud/Schaarschuch, Andreas (2005). Soziale Dienstleistung aus Nutzersicht: Zum Gebrauchswert Sozialer Arbeit. [*Social services from the view of users: on the practical value of social work*]. München: Ernst Reinhardt Verlag.

PowerUs (2013): Mend the Gap. Co-learning methods for a mobilising social work. Ed. by Lund University. Online available http://www.powerus.se/wp-content/uploads/PowerUsBrochure_2013.pdf , last download January 16th, 2016.

Skilton, Christine J. (2011): *Involving Experts by Experience in Assessing Students' Readiness to Practise: The Value of Experiential Learning in Student Reflection and Preparation for Practice.* Social Work Education, Vol. 30, No. 3, pp. 299-311.

Stevens, Simon/Tanner, Denise (2006): *Involving Service Users in the Teaching and Learning of Social Work Students: Reflections on Experience.* Social Work Education, Vol. 25, pp. 360-371.

Utschakowski, Jörg/Sielaff, Gyöngyvér/Bock, Thomas/Winter, Andrea (Hrsg.) (2016). Experten aus Erfahrung: Peerarbeit in der Psychiatrie. [*Experts from experience: peer work in psychiatry*]. Köln: Psychiatrie Verlag.

3.6 Switzerland: First Approaches on an Implementation of Courses with a Gap-Mending Approach

Véronique Eicher and Emanuela Chiapparini

User involvement outside of social work education

In Switzerland, we would like to implement a course with a gap-mending approach at the School of Social Work at the Zurich University of Applied Sciences (ZHAW). However in order to understand these efforts and the possible course, we first present here some information about the Swiss context regarding service user organisation and service user involvement.

Next to social care provided by the state, self-help groups with somatic, psychological, social and other rarer issues are quite prevalent in Switzerland. In 1981, the first centre for self-help was created with the aim of developing and promoting self-help groups, after which several more followed. In 1996, they founded a national association (i.e., "Selbsthilfe Schweiz") to be able to represent the interests of the self-help groups with one voice. Today, "Selbsthilfe Schweiz" comprises all 19 self-help centres in Switzerland with more than 2000 self-help groups (Selbsthilfe Schweiz 2015).

Contrary to self-help groups, user involvement has been slow to become included in public services in health and social work in Switzerland. The area in which user involvement has been most prominent is mental health. The association "Pro Mente Sana" was founded in 1978 and aims to empower people with psychological problems and promotes the recovery approach and peer involvement in Switzerland. They collaborated with the European Leonardo da Vinci project called "Ex-In: Experienced Involvement", running from 2005 to 2007. The goal of this European project was the education and qualification of people with psychiatric experience, so that they may be teachers or professionals in the domain of mental health. Specialists in psychiatry, teachers and people with psychiatric experience from six European countries (i.e., Germany, Netherlands, Norway, Slovenia, Sweden, UK) therefore developed a curriculum for a course for people with psychiatric experience (F.O.K.U.S. 2014).

Based on this project, the association "EX-IN Bern" was founded in March 2010. EX-IN Bern and the Berne University of Applied Sciences (BFH) developed a "Diploma of Advanced Studies", first offered in 2010, which was followed by 15 people with experience in psychiatric facilities. Similar courses are now offered by EX-IN Bern and by Pro Mente Sana. Graduates from these courses have been included in mental health services in different ways, for example as presenters at conferences, as teachers in courses, by leading talk groups in clinics or participating in psychiatric case discussions. Most peers work as "recovery supporters" in clinical institutions, where they lead talk groups and offer one-on-one counselling. Their inclusion is especially important for people who receive involuntary treatment and for their relatives, who benefit from the exchange with peers, who have experience with psychiatric treatment (Ihde-Scholl 2014). In 2013, people with psychiatric experience, who followed the course at BFH or Pro Mente Sana, founded the association "Peer Plus", which is the first organization exclusively reserved for people with psychiatric experience who followed a qualification course. Their aim is to establish and promote qualified peer work in social work and health domains, through a peer pool for example (Peer Plus 2013). Peer involvement has been quite prominent in the domain of prevention. One innovative program is an online juvenile suicide prevention program, called "[U25]", where young adults aged less than 25 may write an email if they experience a crisis or have suicidal thoughts. [U25] explicitly works with peer counsellors, young adults between 17 and 24 who may take a course to become an online peer counsellor for adolescents ([U25] 2015).

Infodrog, the Swiss Office for the Coordination of Addiction Facilities, promotes and supports the diversity, accessibility, and quality of various treatment, counselling and harm reduction services. They have several projects with user involvement, such as the Hepatitis C program "Prevention through peer involvement". In this programme, current drug users take part in a course where they learn about how to minimise infection risks when using needles. Afterwards, they educate other drug users about these risks and how to avoid them, thus multiplying the target audience. These peers are especially important to reach users who are not easy accessible by other health professionals. *Infodrog* specifically emphasises the inclusion of peers already in the development phase of the project (Coste/Droz 2002).

The topic of poverty is less prevalent in service user organisations in Switzerland. Since 2004, Planet13 is an internet café, which has been founded and is run by people living in poverty. It is specifically aimed at people living in poverty so that they have easy and free access to computers and internet and have social contacts (Planet13 2015).

Another type of user involvement is promoted by "Surprise", an independent organisation based in Basel, which aims to help people in difficult situations to get themselves out of these conditions. The organisation exists since 1997 and is funded by own activities and donations of people, companies, and foundations. Surprise offers different activities for people in difficult situations in several German speaking towns of Switzerland: sale of street papers, social city tours, street soccer and street choirs. The main activity – the sale of street papers – is done in coordination with the international network of street papers (INSP). People, who are in financial difficulties sell street papers and earn money for each sold paper. They decide how many hours they work and how many papers they sell and get a daily structure. The social city tours are focused on showing Switzerland from the perspective of people living in poverty. They are developed with people who have lived or still live on the street, who are also the guides on the tours. The street choirs and soccer teams enable social contact without cost and thus facilitate social integration (Surprise 2015).

There are also encouraging advances in user involvement in research. The BFH launched a research project called "PIONEERS – Pioneers of a new paradigm in psychiatric care and supervision at Berne University of Applied Sciences". In this project, users are already included at the development stage of the research project and are hired for the entirety of the project duration (BFH 2015).

Social work education in Switzerland

To the best of our knowledge, user involvement has not yet been realized in social work education programmes. Users have been invited to talk about their experiences, but this was done on the basis of individual talks and presentations. They have not been included in the development of courses or participated in whole courses, either as teachers or students.

After learning about PowerUs and visiting the course in Lund, Sweden (see Chapter 3.1 of this volume), we aim to implement a course with user involvement at the School of Social Work at ZHAW. To put this context, we give some background information on social work education in Switzerland and ZHAW specifically. Social work education in Switzerland consists of a BSc and MSc degree. The BSc degree (180 ECTS) lasts three years (fulltime) and completes with the qualification as social work professional (focus on working directly with clients). The MSc degree (90 ECTS) lasts two years (full time) and qualifies social work professionals for complex conceptual work, research and teaching, as well as leadership positions (SASSA 2007). Currently, most social work professionals have a BSc degree, as the MSc degree exists only since 2008.

At ZHAW, the BSc curriculum consists of basic mandatory modules, advanced optional modules, a 1–year internship and the bachelor-thesis. The advanced optional modules consist of seminars with 7 ECTS and three-consecutive-day seminars of 2 ECTS (Bachelorstudium in Sozialer Arbeit 2015). We developed a concept for a three-consecutive-day seminar with service user involvement, which will be described in the following chapter.

The MSc curriculum is offered in cooperation with Berne University of Applied Sciences, Lucerne University of Applied Sciences and Arts and St. Gallen University of Applied Sciences. It consists of basic mandatory modules, advanced optional modules, a project module and the master-thesis.

Concept of a first course with a gap-mending approach in Zurich

In the previous chapter we presented the structure of the curriculum of the School of Social Work at ZHAW. We developed the concept for a small course with a gap-mending approach as an optional three-consecutive-day seminar of 2 ECTS in the BSc curriculum, called "Empowerment in social work. Encounters of students and service users without the official and contractual relationship". The timeframe is very limited, but the students have a solid theoretical and practical background in social work. In the development of the concept, we were greatly inspired by the course with the gap-mending approach in Lund (see Chapter 3.1), which we visited in spring 2015 (Chiapparini/Eicher 2015) and literature about empowerment, user involvement and social mobilisation (see Chapter 1). The basic idea is that both students and service users learn about the theoretical approach of empowerment and experience empowerment through working together on a topic of social work.

The aim of the course is to offer a learning setting where service users and students of social work can meet one another on an equal basis and exchange their experiences. That is, students and service users have different types of expert knowledge, which they should be able to exchange on equal footing. Additionally, the opportunity to meet each other out of the roles of social worker and service user should enable them to develop concepts of sustainable projects in social work together.

The concept plans for a maximum of 30 participants with approximately 20 BSc students and 10 service users. Service users will be contacted through the network of "Surprise" and so will have a background of poverty in most cases.

The aim of the course is that both service users and students get more sensibility for their respective perspectives and that they learn about the opportunities and challenges of the empowerment approach. It may also be interesting for service users to get a closer look on the curriculum of social work education.

The seminar would be structured in three parts: On the first day, all participants present themselves by answering the questions: Who am I and what is important to me in social work? Additionally, we present theoretical inputs on empowerment, social mobilising and examples of projects with user involvement. The second day focuses on group work between students and service users. They focus on one topic of social work, on which they discuss their perspectives, experiences, and the limits of current social work practice within that topic. The aim is to develop some ideas about projects, which they present on the afternoon of the third and final day. The form of the presentation is open, but should have some creative aspects.

First implementation of the gap-mending approach on a meta-perspective

As we are not yet able to implement the three-consecutive-day seminar in the BSc curriculum, we have introduced the topic of service user involvement from a meta-perspective in an advanced optional module in the MSc curriculum since fall 2015. The module is called "Social problems and conduct of life: Interventions and effects" and the focus is placed on different intervention strategies, such as prevention, control, promotion and empowerment. The topic of empowerment is covered over 8 hours (1 day) and focuses on the service user involvement approach. First, we give an overview on empowerment, social mobilisation and service user involvement. Afterwards, we discuss a paper on the challenges and opportunities of the empowerment approach (Askheim 2003). The afternoon session is dedicated to a specific user involvement project, namely the social city tours of Surprise, which we presented before. First two social work professionals present the development of this project and the challenges in the different project phases. Afterwards, two city tour guides (service users) talk about their background and their experience in working in the project. They specifically discuss opportunities and challenges in working together on a project from the initial development phase to everyday collaboration. The students are able to discuss both with the social work professionals and the service users about their opinion of service user involvement and empowerment. As a thank you, both the social work professionals and service users received a small compensation (a notebook and supermarket vouchers).

Evaluation and critical reflection

After the first implementation of the MSc module "Social problems and conduct of life: Interventions and effects", the evaluation from the students was mostly positive with several valuable suggestions to increase the learning opportunities of the course. In a standardised evaluation of the complete course, the students explicitly mentioned the sessions on empowerment as very important and as an opportunity to get new insights and understandings. However, the students expressed a wish to have a more equal discussion with the service users, in which the service users also ask them questions about their role as social workers. The students also suggested having a common evaluation of the day with the service users, lecturers and students, which would allow more critical reflections and insights.

The social work professionals (the project leader of the social city tours) and the service users (city tour guides) were also satisfied with the launch of the module. The project leader suggested having a longer exchange with the students to be able to reflect the challenges of the empowerment approach more deeply. The service users immediately said that they would like to participate in the next module and would be interested in further projects.

As the lecturers, we evaluated this first module as very successful and we plan to improve the module with the suggestions from the students and service users. In the next implementation of the module, we will reduce the theoretical part on empowerment approach, so that we have more time with the service users and project leaders. As before, we plan to have some time with only the service users and only the project leaders, but we want to include a third common session, in which they reflect on their project together and with the students. More time will also allow for a deeper and more reflective discussion about the different perspectives involved in user involvement projects and social work in general.

Conclusion

Our first experience with the module on the gap-mending approach from a meta-perspective was highly motivating and the feedback from the participants was very encouraging. The service users and project leaders from "Surprise" are highly motivated and we plan to invite them to participate in future modules. As the introduction of a course with a gap-mending approach in the BSc and MSc curricula is quite difficult, we decided to start with a smaller part within an existing module. In time, we hope to be able to implement a longer course with service user involvement. If we are able to implement the BSc module, we will develop the details of the concept of the course together with service users, so that it is adapted to and benefits both the service users and the students. It is also very helpful to be in contact with the network PowerUs to exchange concept ideas and thus advance with the implementation of a course with a gap-mending approach. Additionally, the knowledge and experience of the members of PowerUs is a great source of inspiration.

References

Askheim, Ole Petter (2003): Empowerment as guidance for professional social work: an act of balancing on a slack rope. *European Journal of Social Work* 6 (3), pp. 229-240.

BFH (Berner Fachhochschule) (2015): *Job offer from Berne University of Applied Sciences*. Retrieved on 2.12.2015 from http://www.peerplus.ch/Joomla/images/peerplus/Dokumente/FBG_Peer_10-20.pdf.

Bachelorstudium in Sozialer Arbeit (2015): *Studienführer [study guide]*. Retrieved on 3.12.2015 from https://www.zhaw.ch/storage/shared/sozialearbeit/Studium/ Bachelor/ZHAW-Soziale-Arbeit-Bachelor.pdf.

Chiapparini, Emanuela; Eicher, Véronique (2015): *Einbezug von Adressaten der Sozialen Arbeit ("service users") in die Lehre. Überlegungen zur Umsetzbarkeit der gap-mending Methoden von PowerUs im Rahmen der ZHAW und des Kooperationsmasters. Projektbericht [User involvement in social work education: Reflections about the implementation of gap-mending methods at the Zurich University of Applied Sciences and the cooperation master]*. Zürich. ZHAW Soziale Arbeit.

Coste, Jean-Marie ; Droz, Béatrice (2002): Hepatitis-C-Kampagne: *Projekt Prävention durch Peer-Involvement* [*Intervention project with peer involvement*]. Neuchâtel: Drop-In. Retrieved on 1.12.2015 from http://www.infodrog.ch/index.php/peers-publikationen.html.

F.O.K.U.S. (2014): *Ausbildungsprogramm für Psychiatrie-Erfahrene zur Qualifizierung als Ausbilder und als Genesungsbegleiter. Projektbericht.* [*Continuing education program for users of mental health services to qualify as teacher and recovery guide*] Retrieved on 22.01.2016 from http://docplayer.org/7842656-Ausbildungsprogramm-fuer-psychiatrie-erfahrene-zur-qualifizierung-als-ausbilder-und-als-genesungsbegleiter.html.

Ihde-Scholl, Thomas (2014). *"EX-IN: Vom Ich- zum Wir-Wissen" – ein persönlich gefärbter Erfahrungsbericht.* [*EX-IN: From I to we knowledge. A report of a personal experience*]. Kantonal-Bernischer Hilfsverein für psychisch Kranke. Retrieved on 1.12.2015 from www.be-hilfsverein.ch/publikationen.

Peer Plus (*Fachverband der Expertinnen und Experten durch Erfahrung in psychischser Erschütterung und Genesung*) (2013). *Vereinsstatuten* [*Statutes of the association*]. Zürich.

Planet13 (2015). *Leitbild* [*Guiding principles*]. Basel. Retrieved on 14.1.2015 from https://planet13.ch/wordpress/wp-content/uploads/Leitbild-2.pdf.

SASSA (Fachkonferenz der Fachbereiche Soziale Arbeit der Fachhochschulen der Schweiz) (2007). *Master in Sozialer Arbeit. Rahmenkonzept* [*Master in Social Work. A frame concept*]. Retrieved on 3.12.2015 from http://www.sassa.ch/pdf/Rahmenkonzept%20SASSA%202007-05.pdf.

Selbsthilfe Schweiz (2015): *Jahresbericht 2014* [*Annual report 2014*]. Basel. Retrieved on 1.12.2015 from http://www.selbsthilfeschweiz.ch/shch/de/Ueber-uns/Downloads.html.

Surprise (2015). *Organisation Surprise* [*Organisation of Surprise*]. Basel. Retrieved on 2.12.2015 from http://www.vereinsurprise.ch/organisation/.

[U25] (Online-Beratungsstelle für junge Menschen unter 25 Jahren in Krisen und Suizidgefahr) 2015: *Peer-Ausbildung* [*peer education*]. Winterthur. Retrieved on 1.12.2015 from http://www.u25-bern.ch/index.php/peer-ausbildung-bern.

4. Conclusion: Empowering Service Users and Innovative Learning Settings with Long-Term Effects

Emanuela Chiapparini

This book introduced several examples of courses with the gap-mending approach in social work education in six European countries. The context, the concept, the implementation and the evaluation of these courses vary partly from case to case. However, the central common element of these courses is that service users actively take part as co-partners and valuable contributors in these courses. This goes beyond respecting service users as a person with their own experience and knowledge. The partnership between service users and students of social work constitutes a core element of the different implementations of the gap-mending approach developed at the University in Lund. The gap-mending approach is based on the concept of user involvement, which has a strong relevance both in the International Federation of Social Workers and in the individual countries. The examples of courses described in this book emphasise the fact that the concept of user involvement is not a tokenistic involvement or a rhetorical expression, but rather one that has been successfully implemented. One crucial element of the evaluations demonstrates how important the knowledge and experience of both service users and students of social work is to increase fruitful developments of projects with a high impact on social practices. A process of a reciprocal and deeper understanding of both service users' and social work students' perspectives started with these courses. Consequently, this has an influence on the future of both service users and students of social work. Furthermore, the examples contribute to the development and better understanding of social work.

The following conclusion highlights some key issues and main elements through all specified courses and mentions some differences too. Thereby, it connects these findings to the theoretical background of user involvement and outlines future perspectives.

From an Explorative Learning Process to a Concept of Innovative Projects for Social Challenges

Learning and teaching within a gap-mending approach includes learning settings where service users and students of social work meet. In this context, they learn about theoretical concepts and how to develop a project to resolve social challenges. The number of participants and the duration of each course vary depending on the needs of the participants, of social institutions and the framework of the universities and the context of the courses. However, in all pedagogical concepts of the courses presented in this book, the knowledge and experience of the service users are considered as important as those of the students of social work. Furthermore, in all chapters it is common that the participants of the courses and the lecturers have a high commitment to meet on the same level as far as possible. They pay attention to different attitudes, which means for example that they need to be able to and are willing to listen. Regarding this learning process, the authors in this book made similar theoretical reflections:

The authors of Chapter 3.3 mentioned the learning concept of "partnership" (Thompson 2003) and participation as being an "active ingredient in effective partnership working" (Thompson 2003). Accordingly, the authors of Chapter 3.2 base their courses on a cooperative learning process. The emotional aspect is highlighted in Chapter 3.1, where the authors refer to the research study of the development of students' empathy in medical education. The results show the importance that students do not only acquire a theoretical knowledge about their patient but need to be touched emotionally by meetings with the patients and subsequently have to reflect these experiences. In Chapter 3.4, the concept of "creativity" in social work education (Burgess/Lawrence 2007; Eadie/Lymbery 2007) is mentioned. In this learning concept, different perspectives and experiences are included in the learning process in order to encourage thinking "outside the box" (Burgess/Lawrence 2007: 2), which facilitates the achievement of effective and good practice in social work.

In sum, it can be said that these learning concepts promote good practice in social work by emphasising the importance of personal experience, hands-on, explorative learning and by presenting different perspectives on social challenges. The explorative learning concept is especially elaborated and established in international social work courses (e.g. community-based participatory model by Fischer and Grettenberger (2015)). This concept attaches great importance to including awareness, practice skill development and enhanced competence regarding global and intercultural issues.

Furthermore, an important element of the learning process is that the participation in the courses is voluntary and that both service users and students of social work are as much as possible outside their typical role.

This is a challenge and all authors underline the important function of the lecturer as supporter, moderator and intervener, which requires a non-classical and academic role of lecturer. With regard to this, the authors of Chapter 3.2 give the useful advice to pay attention to avoid prejudice, such as the notion that service users are not able to take criticism or that students of social work are always helpers. If these attitudes or tensions generated by previous negative experience manifest themselves in the working groups, the lecturer needs to recognise them and intervene. This implies good social competence and a high work load for the lecturers, but also for the students themselves.

A central element in each course, mostly at the beginning, is to have enough time to get to know each other as human beings. Different methods of becoming acquainted with each other are described in each chapter.

In the courses in Sweden and Norway, both service users and students of social work get ECTS-credits if they meet all requirements for passing the courses. To obtain permission to get ECTS-credits for service users is a major challenge in most countries. In England, for instance, where user involvement is compulsory in social work education, the authors make a major effort to award ECTS-credits to service users. However, already the fact that they are able to participate in academic courses at universities is appreciated by most service users because it boosts their self-esteem. This is underlined clearly by the evaluations of Norway and Sweden.

The above mentioned elements of gap-mending courses will contribute to creating conditions in which service users and students of social work are on a level playing field.

Kristiansen and Heule prefer the participation of service users with different backgrounds and from different service user organisations, which is helpful for developing concepts of projects with a variety of perspectives.

Developing concepts for innovative projects is another key element of courses with a gap-mending approach. It is important that the project is based on a social challenge. In most courses, the service users and students of social work choose the issues and develop the project on their own, but there are some exceptions. In Germany, the students and the lecturers of social work choose and develop challenging topics and issues, which are then discussed with selected service users before the start of the two-day seminar. In other cases, the issues are proposed by social services. In an English Family Centre, this was initiated because of an existing barrier between service users and students of social work. Courses in Denmark, for instance, are also initiated by social services and political authorities.

The prevailing element of all courses is a strong motivation of students and service users due to the development of and participation in projects. In Sweden, the project concepts are evaluated by a jury with representatives from the political authorities, social services, user organisations and the audience. After this public event, the students and lecturers evaluate the feedback.

Also courses from other countries present similar products at the end of the courses, e.g. a film or a workshop. Especially in Denmark, an innovation camp took place with 60 participants from user organisations, practitioners, local government authorities, private service providers and participants of the gap-mending course. The findings and proposals of the gap-mending course were presented and discussed together on an equal level.

From Involving Services Users to Decreasing Social Inequality

In Sweden or Norway, the concept of user involvement is established in social work education through internships, through invitations of service users to visit classes or through visiting social services and projects, for instance. However, these occasions do not necessarily give the opportunity for a reciprocal understanding of both service users and social workers, which is essential for achieving long-term effects (cf. Chapter 3.2) or improving critical thinking on a sociopolitical level (cf. Chapters 3.1 and 3.3). In order to achieve this, it is crucial to study and work on a project together during a longer period of time and not only during selective moments or individual days (cf. Chapters 3.1-3.4). A theoretical and socio-political overview is clarified particularly in Chapter 3.1 and Chapter 3.3. They point to a link between the gap-mending courses and the redistribution of power in social work practices. Both contributions clearly underline how courses with a gap-mending approach are able to deal with social conditions of inequality more intensely, to mobilise service users and to start developing long-term solutions for social problems.

User involvement is an approach that is more common in English-speaking countries. However, in Switzerland, the contact with service users during the education of social work is very important, even if it does not run under the name of "user involvement". In Germany, the education of social work has a longer academic tradition than in Switzerland, which makes it harder for Germany to introduce courses with user involvement. Both countries have implemented courses with a gap-mending approach in their existing modules with some adaptations such as a short period of time during which service users and students of social work learn and work together (cf. Chapters 3.5 and 3.6).

The terminology "service users" explained in the introduction of this book is used by all authors. In an interdisciplinary context, the short term "users" is more appropriate, as it is argued in Chapter 3.4. In courses, the service users are called students from service user organisations, external students or just students in order to underline the equal positon of all participants in the courses.

It is important to reflect about the terminology of "user involvement" or "service user" to be aware of the implicit, language-related concepts and their limits (cf. Chapter 2). The examples of the courses show that it is important to clarify the terminology in order to eliminate social inequality. Thereby, service users are given the opportunity to be on eye level with the students of social work as much as possible and to work and study together as equal partners during a course that lasts several weeks.

Most of the universities dispose of a large network of user organisations for recruiting service user students. In countries such as Germany and Switzerland, where there are not many user organisations, the recruitment of service users for a course is a great challenge. Service user organisations in Norway, Sweden or England are more common and often run by the service users themselves. Nevertheless, there are groups who are not represented by service user organisations and who are not included enough in endeavours of user involvement (cf. Chapter 3.1) or are not eligible for benefit (cf. Chapter 3.3). For these groups, further efforts and developments of user involvement are required.

In Germany and Switzerland, user organisations are more present in the field of psychology and health care than in the field of social work. Furthermore, the service user organisations are often managed by professionals, as for instance the service user organisations "Surprise" and "EX-IN". The concept of a user-led "organisation" is more common in the numerous self-help groups. A self-help group is commonly considered as less proactive concerning social change and it is by definition a group and not an organisation.

Evaluations: Research-Based and Practice-Based Impact

There is a high demand for results from evaluations of gap-mending courses to evidence their impact on service users, students of social work and on the practice of social work.

The courses presented in this book were assessed both through research-based and practice-based evaluations. The methods of evaluation were questionnaires, group discussions, discussions and written reflections about learning effects, which were conducted with students of social work and students of service user organisations. The notable results and some challenges of gap-mending courses are described in each chapter and constitute a first evaluation of courses with a gap-mending approach within one volume.

With the long experience of gap-mending courses at the Lund University, these courses demonstrate in a unique way their impact on social work practice: Service users founded new service user organisations. They also elaborated concepts in gap-mending courses, which received funding so that they could subsequently be implemented and applied in social work practice. The service users were invited as guest lecturers or tutors to courses or as participants to national and international congresses of social work.

The first evaluation of long-term effects was conducted by the Norwegian authors (cf. Chapter 3.2). They used the method of retrospective interviews of service users in group discussions. Thus, they found a long-term effect, which they discussed under five headlines: 1) an experience of involvement, 2) an awareness of labelling, 3) an increase in self-confidence and the empowerment of role-changing, 4) the importance of gaining the understanding and cooperation of each other, and 5) increasing values such as being part of a community or obtaining self-respect.

Another positive practice-based outcome of each course is based on the fact that they are continually developed and implemented and that there is great demand for such courses.

The above mentioned research and practice-based evaluations of gap-mending courses provide answers to the four crucial questions by Schön (2016: 31):

- How should one proceed with these efforts?
- Which methods produce the most favourable outcomes?
- What does it mean to be in a user role? Is it a stigma or an improvement?
- How does this enhanced knowledge affect students' work and attitudes once they become social workers?

Additionally, the mentioned evaluations of courses with a gap-mending approach can be classified, with certain restrictions, into Schön's very appropriate categories for evaluating user involvement in social work, education and practice. (Schön 2016: 31):

- outcome-focused research on methods and levels of user participation
- users' perceptions of the quality of these activities
- the effect of these activities on a user's quality of life.

It can thus be concluded that the contributions of all authors of this book counteract the "lack of evidence based knowledge" (Schön 2016: 31) of user involvement in social work, education and practice.

However, there is a great need for further research-based and practice-based evaluations especially to evidence long-term outcomes of gap-mending courses by service users and students of social work. The authors of this book emphasise this demand for future research as well.

In conclusion, all authors have shown how courses with a gap-mending approach achieve empowerment among socially excluded groups and promote learning processes in different socio-political contexts as well as varying framework of universities. These courses reveal the views and needs of both service users and social workers and provide meeting points and platforms, where both groups can develop innovative projects in the field of social work. There are different stages of development of these courses, which is at the same time a promising outlook towards a continuing and increasing advancement of the gap-mending approach.

References

Burgess, H./Laurance, J. (2007): Reflections on Creativity in Social Work and Social Work Education Disciplinary Perspectives on Creativity in Higher Education, [online] 13 Oct 2008. Available from: http://www.heacademy.ac.uk/creativity.htm [accessed on 8th January 2016].

Eadie, T./Lymbery, M. (2007): Promoting Creative Practice Through Social Work Education. In: Social Work Education, 26 (7), pp. 670-683.

Fisher, C. M./Grettenberger Susan E. (2015): Community-Based Participatory Study Abroad: A Proposed Model for Social Work Education. In: Journal of Social Work Education, 51 (3), pp. 566-582.

Schön, U.-K. (2016): User Involvement in Social Work and Education-A Matter of Participation? In: Journal of evidence-informed social work, 13 (1), pp. 21-33.

Thompson, N. (2003): Promoting equality: challenging discrimination and oppression, second edition, Basingstoke: Palgrave Macmillan.

The contributors

Liv Altmann is an assistant professor at Lillehammer University College at Faculty of Education and Social Work. Her main interests in both teaching and practical work are facilitating empowerment and service user involvement. Liv Altmann worked with parents with children with disabilities for many years.
Email: liv.altmann@hil.no

Ole Petter Askheim, is a professor at Lillehammer University College at Faculty of Education and Social work. His main interest is user involvement and empowerment for service users and he has written books and articles about the issue. He has been working theoretically with the concepts and has shown a special interest in how to implement empowerment for disabled people and persons with mental health problems.
Email: Ole-Petter.Askheim@hil.no

Peter Beresford, OBE, is a professor of Citizen Participation, the University of Essex and Emeritus Professor of Social Policy, Brunel University London. He has a longstanding involvement in issues of participation as writer, researcher, activist and educator. Peter Beresford is Co-Chair of the service users' and disabled people's organisation, Shaping Our Lives, and a long term user of mental health services. His latest book is All Our Welfare: Towards participatory social policy, Policy Press, 2016.
Email: peter.beresford3@btopenworld.com

Helen Casey is the course leader of the social work degree programme at New College Durham. She has over ten years of experience as a lecturer and prior to this, ten years as a social worker in hospital and community settings. In both education and practice Helen has promoted service user and carer involvement throughout her work. She is currently undertaking research to explore the impact of service user and carer involvement in health and care professional education.
Email: Helen.Casey@newdur.ac.uk

Emanuela Chiapparini, PhD, is a senior researcher in national and international research projects and a lecturer at the Institute of Childhood, Youth and Family of the School of Social Work at Zurich University of Applied Sciences. She is a sociologist of youth research. Her focus topics are social problems and inequality, informal peer groups, civic engagement, participation, user involvement and cooperation in all-day schools.
Email: Emanuela.Chiapparini@zhaw.ch

Véronique Eicher, PhD, is head of the master degree program at the Zurich University of Applied Sciences. Her research interests include transitions in young adulthood and she teaches research methods in social work. She is interested in the topic of user involvement in teaching, research and practice.
Email: veronique.eicher@zhaw.ch

Tove Hasvold is an assistant professor at Lillehammer University College at Faculty of Education and Social Work. She has worked for many years with children and families at risk. Her focus of interest is how empowerment can be promoted by building on individual and environmental strengths and resources.
Email: ove.hasvold@hil.no

Camusa Hatt, M.A., is an associate professor and leader of in national and international research projects at the Metropolitan University College. She has years of experience in teaching, developing, implementing and evaluating interprofessional education (IPE). She has a keen interest in the development of shared knowledge and pedagogical facilitation of interprofessional education and interprofessional collaboration.
Email: caha@phmetropol.dk

Thomas Heidenreich, Prof, PhD, Dipl.-Psych., is a professor and vice dean at the Faculty of Social Work, Health Care and Nursing Sciences of Esslingen University of Applied Sciences. His main areas of interest are counselling and therapeutic approaches in social work. Together with Marion Laging, he has been developed and conducted Service User Involvement seminars and activities since 2014.
Email: thomas.heidenreich@hs-esslingen.de

Cecilia Heule is a social work teacher at Lund University in Sweden. She has been working with community development in Holland and in Sweden. Since 2004 she has been developing gap-mending methods in the education of social workers together with Arne Kristiansen. She was the coordinator of the international network PowerUs as it developed in a partnership with partners from Norway and the UK in 2011. Her research is about social mobilisation, boundaries in professional social work and collation between social workers and service users.
Email: cecilia.heule@soch.lu.se

Marion Laging, Prof, PhD, she is social worker and social pedagogue and has been professor since 2005 at the faculty of Social Work, Health Care and Nursing Science. Marion Laging is vice dean and head of the Bachelor Degree Program of Social Work. Her main interests include participative approaches in theory, practice and education. Together with Thomas Heidenreich she has been developed and conducted Service User Involvement seminars and activities since 2014.
Email: Marion.Laging@hs-esslingen.de

John MacDonough is a senior lecturer in social work at London South Bank University, where he leads on the involvement and participation of service users and carers throughout the delivery of social work education at the university. He is a practicing social worker with over twenty years' experience of working with young people and adults with learning difficulties, and currently helps to run two social enterprises run by and for adults with learning difficulties. John also chairs a charity working with street children in the Philippines where gap-mending principles are used to engage and empower communities.
Email: macdonoj@lsbu.ac.uk

Arne Kristiansen, PhD, is senior lecturer at Lund University (Sweden). His current research interests include substance abuse, homelessness and service user involvement. He has spent several years working as a social worker. He works closely with various service user organisations, which he involves both in social work education and in research projects. With Cecilia Heule he developed and started the first course with gap-mending approach in 2005.
Email: arne.kristiansen@soch.lu.se

Ann Rasmussen, M.Sc., is project manager and special advisor, Metropolitan University College. She has a broad experience and interest in user involvement as a valuable method of innovating both in public services and welfare technologies. User involvement has been an integrated part of her recent innovation projects, which promote collaboration – or gap-mending – across the public and private sector, and across different professions.
Email: annr@phmetropol.dk

Malin Widerlöv is the founder and chairwoman of the service user organization "Maskrosföräldrar" ("Dandelion") in Sweden. She is a tutor and a guest lecturer of the mobilisation course at the School of Social Work (University Lund, Sweden). She participated in the European Association of School of Social Work (EASSW) conference 2015 in Milan with the paper "How to Empower a Collapsed Parenthood". She was the presenter of the film "Mend the Gap – A Challenge for Social Work Education" (2015) at the same conference, giving an overview of the gap-mending courses in England, Sweden and Norway to a large audience.
Email: malin.widerlov@gmail.com

GPSR Authorized Representative: Easy Access System Europe, Mustamäe tee
50, 10621 Tallinn, Estonia, gpsr.requests@easproject.com

www.ingramcontent.com/pod-product-compliance
Lightning Source LLC
Chambersburg PA
CBHW071715020426
42333CB00017B/2282